SonGames 2004
Assemblies and Skits Production Guide

Gospel Light

How to make clean copies from this book

You may make copies of portions of this book with a clean conscience if

- you (or someone in your organization) are the original purchaser;
- you are using the copies you make for a noncommercial purpose (such as teaching or promoting your ministry) within your church or organization;
- you follow the instructions provided in this book.

However, it is ILLEGAL for you to make copies if

- you are using the material to promote, advertise or sell a product or service other than for ministry fund-raising;
- you are using the material in or on a product for sale; or
- you or your organization are not the original purchaser of this book.

By following these guidelines you help us keep our products affordable.

Thank you,

Gospel Light

Permission to make photocopies of or to reproduce by any other mechanical or electronic means in whole or in part any designated* page, illustration or activity in this book is granted only to the original purchaser and is intended for noncommercial use within a church or other Christian organization. None of the material in this book may be reproduced for any commercial promotion, advertising or sale of a product or service. Sharing of the material in this book with other churches or organizations not owned or controlled by the original purchaser is also prohibited. All rights reserved.

*Pages with the following notation can be legally reproduced:
© 2004 Gospel Light. Permission to photocopy granted. SonGames 2004 *Assemblies and Skits Production Guide*

Scripture quotations are taken from the *Holy Bible, New International Version*®. Copyright © 1973, 1978, 1984 by International Bible Society. Used by permission of Zondervan Publishing House. All rights reserved.

Gospel Light Vacation Bible School

Founder, Henrietta Mears • **Publisher Emeritus,** William T. Greig • **Publisher, Children's Curriculum and Resources,** Lynnette Pennings, M.A. • **Senior Consulting Publisher,** Dr. Elmer L. Towns • **Managing Editor,** Sheryl Haystead • **Senior Editor,** Kim Fiano • **Senior Consulting Editors,** Wesley Haystead, M.S.Ed., Christy Weir • **Senior Editor, Biblical and Theological Issues,** Bayard Taylor, M.Div. • **Skit Writer,** Judy Nyren • **Editor,** Karen McGraw • **Associate Editor,** Heather Kempton • **Contributing Editors,** Cyndi Lunden, Sherri Martin • **Senior Designer,** Carolyn Thomas

© 2004 Gospel Light, Ventura, CA 93006. All rights reserved. Printed in the U.S.A.

Contents

Opening and Closing Assemblies 4

SonGames Skits Overview 5

Publicity Ideas 5

Casting 6

Rehearsal 6

Characters 7

Stadium Backdrop and Constructed Props 9

Stage Setup 11

Stadium Backdrop Pattern 14

Props 15

Session 1
Opening Assembly/Skit 16
Closing Assembly 19

Session 2
Opening Assembly/Skit 20
Closing Assembly 23

Session 3
Opening Assembly/Skit 24
Closing Assembly 27

Session 4
Opening Assembly/Skit 28
Closing Assembly 31

Session 5
Opening Assembly/Skit 32
Closing Assembly 35

SonGames Closing Ceremony 36
Closing Program Skit Script 37

Opening and Closing Assemblies

Opening Assemblies

Each day at SonGames begins and ends with an assembly for children in grades 1 through 6, led by the VBS Director or a volunteer. Each day, children will learn about being a part of God's team. Each of these concepts is represented by a daily motto and symbol to be displayed in front of the assembly room. Use Motto Pennants (available from Gospel Light) or reproduce the patterns found in *Elementary Teaching and Decorating Resources* onto poster board. Every opening assembly features a skit designed to catch the children's attention and introduce the daily Bible focus from the book of Acts (see "SonGames Skits Overview" on p. 5).

Gathering

Here are some tips for getting your students into and situated in the assembly hall:

⚽ Have classes parade in and around the assembly hall (like the Olympic Parade of Athletes) before sitting down.

⚽ Have classes sit with teachers and helpers.

⚽ Seat younger children in the front of the assembly hall.

⚽ Have a helper for each team hold a sign to the group or post signs in areas where groups sit or gather. Not only will this identify each group for activities during the assemblies, but it will also help latecomers know where to find their classes.

Video Highlights

To enhance the atmosphere of a sports broadcast, skits for Sessions 2-5 provide an opportunity to show the video clips from the previous session of SonGames. Ask a volunteer or someone from your church's video department to shoot footage of activities each day. A volunteer or the actor portraying sportscaster Joe Gabbyola in the skits can provide commentary of the action and/or conduct interviews with kids, staff and helpers from your church's SonGames. These segments should be edited to run for no more than three to five minutes. Project the video on a wall or screen in your assembly room at the time indicated in each skit or as students gather in the assembly hall. (Note: In Skit 4 you may also choose to show video of Stella Swift falling during her race and then crawling to the finish line.)

Instead of a video, you may choose to prepare a slide show.

NOTE: The skit video does not provide opportunities to show video (or slide) highlights from previous session. If you choose to show the skits on the *Teaming Up at SonGames Skit Video* instead of performing live skits, show video highlights as children gather in the assembly hall or during your Opening or Closing Assembly.

Closing Assemblies

Each closing assembly reviews the memory verse and again reinforces the focus before dismissing children with a tantalizing glimpse of the next day. You may choose to have preschool children attend the assemblies, or various skit characters can visit the individual early-childhood classrooms to lead children in a review of the memory verse and the session's focus.

SonGames Medals

During the Closing Assembly, give SonGames Medals to the teachers or other representatives of the top three classes judged to be the best in a serious or silly category. Here are some suggested categories: most students on time, singing the loudest, most visitors, most members with funny hairstyles, most students bringing their Bibles, most students wearing the same color, memorizing the most verses, increasing the most in attendance, most members wearing sports uniforms, etc.

Make three medals from poster board and blue ribbon or crepe-paper streamers. Paint one gold, another silver and the last medal bronze. Or see instructions for making medals in *Gold-Medal Crafts for Kids*.

Set up the Medalists' Podium to the side of the stage (see "Decorating Ideas" in *Elementary Teaching and Decorating Resources*). Announce the awards and then play music from SonGames cassette/CD as the medals are distributed. The teacher or other representative for the third-place class stands on the lowest level and receives a bronze medal. The representative for the second-place class stands on the next higher level and receives a silver medal. The representative for the first-place class stands on the highest level and receives a gold medal.

NOTE: Make sure that each class is recognized at least once during the week.

(Optional: Instead of awarding three medals, have only one medal or prize that a member of the class could carry as they travel to centers and assemblies. Instead of a medal, consider these suggested prizes: a large inflatable ball, a Motto Pennant or reproduction attached to a long stick, a torch prop, a piece of sporting equipment, a trophy, a sneaker attached to a board and spray-painted gold, etc.)

SonGames Skits Overview

The skits take place at the SonGames Sports Stadium. Joe Gabbyola, a television sportscaster, has come to cover the competitions and do a personal profile on the athletic team from the tiny country of Smallvania. It is the country's first time to compete in the events. Each Smallvanian athlete—Tumbelina Turnover, Brutus Liftsalot and Stella Swift—competes in a different sport; but they learn to work together as a team for their country.

Children will be delighted to watch the characters as they prepare for and compete in their events. Each skit is specifically written to illustrate the focus of the day's lesson. The conversation in the summary at the end of each skit will help your students make the connection between the skit and the lesson focus. The other components of the assemblies (Bible Memory Verse, Prayer, Song, Review, etc.) will also reinforce the lesson focus.

HELPFUL HINT: Check out the bulletin boards at www.gospellightvbs.com. These discussion groups give you the opportunity to exchange skit production tips with directors from all over the United States and Canada. Discover proven methods to set the stage and get your actors up and running.

Publicity Ideas

The skits are excellent devices for building excitement and encouraging participation in the weeks before your VBS begins. Once children meet Joe Gabbyola, Tumbelina, Brutus and Stella, they can't wait to see them again! Most children actually enjoy the skits more at VBS if they have already seen one or two before they come. Consider the ideas below that many churches have found effective.

Before VBS

⚽ **Present Skits to Congregation**—Get the attention of your entire congregation by presenting all or part of one skit during a worship service or other congregational event. You may wish to write your own promotional skit using the skit characters. Seeing a skit will help build interest among children and will motivate adults to volunteer their services.

⚽ **Present Skits to Sunday School Classes**—Have the actors visit children's and adults' Sunday School classes instead of, or in addition to, presenting a skit during a worship service. Actors can hand out promotional materials (flyers, registration cards, etc.) and make announcements as the skit characters.

⚽ **Present Skits in Parks and Neighborhoods**—The skits can also capture the attention of unchurched families. Any setting where children and families gather provides an opportunity for a brief skit and announcement. Play music from the *SonGames* cassette/CD to help draw a crowd. Distribute information about the upcoming VBS and personally invite listeners to attend.

After VBS

⚽ **Present Skits at the Closing Program or on the Next Sunday**—Unchurched people may feel uncomfortable coming to church after VBS is over, but the skit characters are proven bridge builders at this crucial time. Announce that the SonGames skit characters will be at the Closing Ceremony—or at church next Sunday—and that they will be looking for all the SonGames teams to be there, too. When made a part of your invitation to children and parents, these characters will help your visitors feel more comfortable about attending.

Casting

Choose seven people to play the parts of Tumbelina Turnover, Stella Swift, Brutus Liftsalot, Joe Gabbyola, Stagehand, Director and Announcer. The script calls for two females, two males and three roles that are not gender specific. However, feel free to adapt any or all of the roles to accommodate the gender of your actors. Choose people who have a sense of humor and some dramatic ability. They need to commit to rehearse in order to be fully prepared for each skit.

Skits 4 and 5 each feature three additional characters. The minor parts of the runners in Skit 4 and the judges in Skit 5 can be played by VBS children—a fun way to use your students' acting talents and add interest and excitement to your assembly time. Children are always interested in either being on stage or watching their friends perform.

Making Your Characters Come Alive

The key to making your skit characters come alive is to have each one develop a clearly defined personality. The students will get to know the characters and enjoy anticipating how each one might react in different situations. Development of a character includes:

⚽ **Movements**—Each actor should practice movements that reflect his or her character's personality, such as a way of walking, a stance, a gesture of the hands or a strong, emphatic way of entering and leaving the stage. For example, Tumbelina is very excited and animated. She seems incapable of standing still and tends to jump up and down and clap her hands enthusiastically. Stella is focused on her training and frequently stretches or runs in place rather than standing still. Brutus flexes his muscles and Joe smoothes his hair or fixes his tie.

Actors should always remember to face the audience when they speak and never to cross in front of another actor when he or she is speaking.

⚽ **Speech**—Each actor should speak in a voice that accentuates his or her character's personality. Each actor should also take note of phrases that are important or typical of his or her character and practice saying them in ways that will be memorable to the children without sacrificing clarity. For example, Joe Gabbyola speaks with the well-practiced intonation of a seasoned professional broadcaster. He also loves to talk about his own glory days as an athlete or to spout off sports clichés.

⚽ **Costumes**—Enhance each character with an individualized costume (see pp. 7-8). If you don't have all of the suggested items, substitutions can easily be made. Thrift stores, yard sales and the closets of congregation members are good sources of inexpensive (or free) costumes.

Rehearsal

Rehearsal is essential to the success of your skits. Actors must be totally familiar with characterizations, spoken lines and positions onstage. Confident, well-prepared actors will present the message of the skit clearly and powerfully. Rehearsal also allows actors the opportunity to be creative and flexible. They can add their own expressions, gestures or movements to customize their character.

Have someone watch each rehearsal and make comments. This person should observe if actors are positioning themselves correctly on the stage and are speaking slowly, loudly and clearly, with appropriate expressions and gestures.

The *Teaming Up at SonGames Skit Video* can help you prepare for your live performances. A fully staged production of all five skits on this video provides ideas for the backdrop, props and costumes. The video can also help your volunteer actors develop facial expressions, vocal inflections and gestures. (You may even choose to show the video instead of performing live skits.)

© 2004 Gospel Light. Permission to photocopy granted. SonGames 2004 *Assemblies and Skits Production Guide*

Characters

Tumbelina Turnover is a perky and spirited gymnast competing in the new sport of freestyle gymnastics. She's more an artist than an athlete. Ever optimistic, she cheers her teammates on enthusiastically. She tends to skip instead of walk wherever she goes. Tumbelina relies heavily on her emotions to help her "feel the moment," and after a disastrous routine, she discovers it's important to listen to good advice.

NOTE: On each Smallvanian athlete's uniform is the acronym H.E.L.P. U.S. The letters stand for their team motto: *Hope, Endurance, Loyalty, Peace*—United Smallvania. The uniforms should be the same color with letters in a contrasting color.

Brutus Liftsalot is a weight lifter who honed his skills working on the farm back home. He is very strong physically but a big softie emotionally. He cares about others and is ready to lend a helping hand when needed. When Brutus becomes homesick, he learns there are other kinds of strength in addition to the purely physical.

Tumbelina
T-shirt
exercise pants
ponytail
6-foot (1.8-m) length of 2-inch (5-cm) ribbon attached to dowel

Brutus
sweat suit padded with foam balls, shoulder pads, batting, etc.

NOTE: It is not necessary that the actor portraying Tumbelina be a gymnast or even particularly graceful. Performing the suggested moves badly but with great spirit and enthusiasm will only add to the humor.

NOTE: The script calls for physical humor from all the athletic characters. Though none of the action is very demanding physically, the actors playing those roles should be comfortable with pantomime and exaggerated facial expressions and gestures.

Stella Swift is the most successful, most competitive athlete on the Smallvanian team. She is a runner who is expected to win in the 200-, 400- and 800-meter races. Stella is serious, focused, experienced and outwardly confident. Though she comes to the SonGames convinced that she doesn't need any help from her teammates, Stella learns she can trust and rely on them, and by doing so, she becomes a better athlete and a happier person.

Joe Gabbyola is a professional sportscaster and acts as a sort of master of ceremonies. He has a tendency to spout sports sayings at every opportunity. Joe is also very self-important and jumps at the chance to talk about himself. His reporting helps set the stage for each day's skit and his interviews help us get to know the other characters more intimately.

Stella
warm-up suit
running shoes

Joe
slacks
dress shirt
and tie
suit jacket
press pass with
large safety pin

Stagehand appears at the beginning of Skits 1-3 and Skit 5, sprucing Joe up or doing other preparatory tasks before the camera goes on. There are no lines for this character.

Director and **Announcer** speak offstage. These characters are never seen onstage and may be two offstage actors, one offstage actor doing two different voices or you may use recorded voices.

Three Additional Runners appear in Skit 4 and race against Stella in slow motion. Three Judges appear in Skit 5. These roles provide good opportunities for children from your VBS to perform. Though there are no lines to be spoken by these characters, be sure to arrange practice time so that they know what to do and where to go during the skit.

© 2004 Gospel Light. Permission to photocopy granted. SonGames 2004 *Assemblies and Skits Production Guide*

Stadium Backdrop and Constructed Props

A large painted scene of the SonGames Sports Stadium will add color and provide an interesting backdrop for the skits. Talk with someone in your church or community who is familiar with painting backdrop scenes and determine which material would work best for your backdrop (paper, fabric, cardboard, muslin and wood react differently to various kinds of paints). Make your stadium backdrop at least 8x10 feet (2.4x3 m), preferably the same width as your stage.

Photocopy the Stadium Backdrop Pattern (see p. 14) onto a transparency. Use a transparency projector to enlarge the design onto your backdrop material and trace the design with pen or pencil. Paint background colors first, adding details after the background has dried.

Runner's Torch
Bend a large sheet of poster board into a cone. Staple or tape securely. Spray with metallic paint. Crumple tissue paper or newspaper into the bottom of the torch as shown in sketch. Insert a flashlight and add additional crumpled paper to hold flashlight upright. Cut, twist, flare and shape red, yellow and orange tissue paper to resemble flames. Staple flames to rim of cone.

Folded Letter
On a large sheet of butcher paper print the following in letters large enough to be read by the audience: "Dear Brutus, We are so proud of you! We know you will do your best. We love you. Your Family. P.S. Here is your cell-phone charger. You left it in the barn." Fold letter in half five or six times.

Participant Tags
Cut four 12-inch (30.5-cm) squares of felt. Using a permanent marker, print the following country names, one on each felt square: "Smallvania," "Somalia," "Sri Lanka" and "Slovakia."

Flip Sign
On a 5x15-inch (12.5x38-cm) piece of poster board, print "Much More" on one side and "Grease" on the other side.

Country Placards
On three sheets of 9x12-inch (23x30.5-cm) construction paper, print the following country names in large block letters: "U.S.A.," "Japan" and "Italy."

Scorecards
On each of six sheets of construction paper, print the following numbers large enough to fill the sheet: "1," "2," "1," "10," "10" and "10." On the back of each sheet, print the same number just large enough so that the actor holding the card can read it.

"ER" Patches
On patches of felt or other fabric, print "ER" in large letters. Make sure patches are sized appropriately to change the letters on Stella's and Brutus's uniforms from H.E.L.P. U.S. to H.E.L.P.ERS.

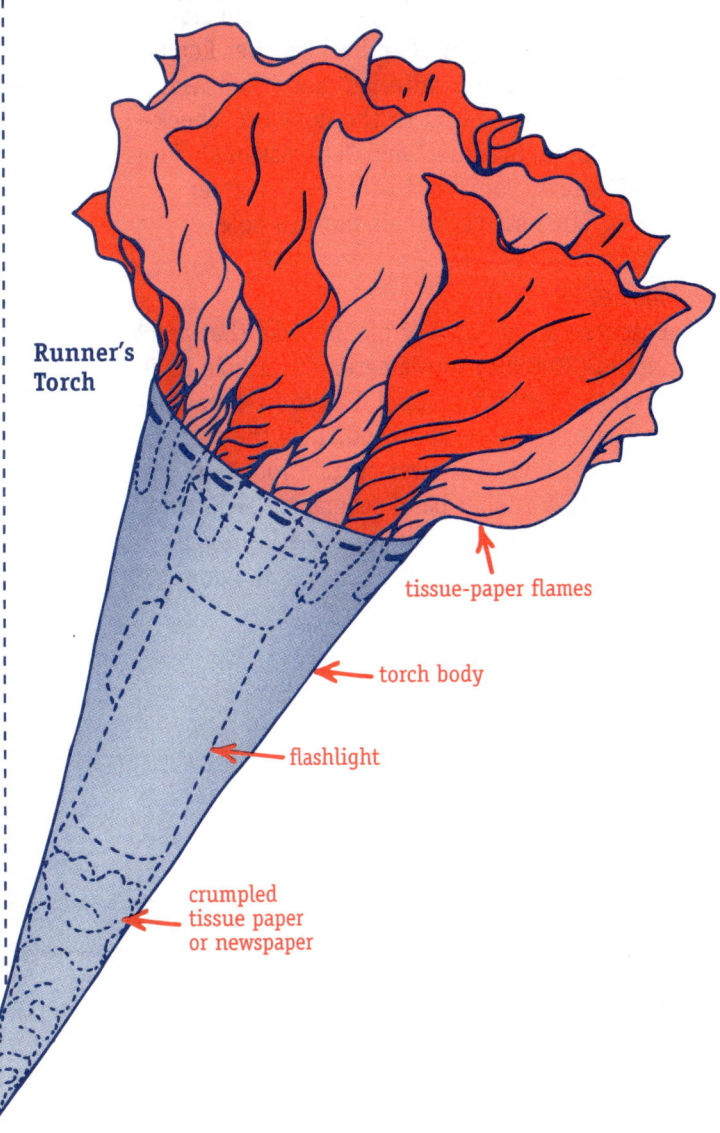

Runner's Torch
- tissue-paper flames
- torch body
- flashlight
- crumpled tissue paper or newspaper

© 2004 Gospel Light. Permission to photocopy granted. SonGames 2004 *Assemblies and Skits Production Guide*

Standing Torch

Cut several flame shapes from red-, yellow- and orange-colored transparency film (used to make overhead transparencies or report covers). Tape transparent flame shapes to the inside rim of a torchère floor lamp. If you have a floor lamp that uses a shade, remove the shade and cut a hole in the bottom of a large plastic bowl that you have painted silver. Drop bowl over bulb and tape to lamp pole and attach flames as described above. For a nice effect, use a red or yellow bulb.
Note: Do NOT use a halogen bulb. Instead, use a floor lamp with regular household lightbulbs. Use a low-watt (no more than 40 watts) bulb.

SPECIAL EFFECTS OPTION: Purchase a flame illusion from the special-effects division of a theatrical supply company. Plug in or turn on at the appropriate moment.

Sign Post

Place a 5-foot (1.5-m) pole in a Christmas tree holder or umbrella stand and secure. Print the following phrases on thin poster board signs: "Check-In," "Sports Stadium," "Locker Room," "Concessions," "Dormitories" and "First Aid." Draw arrows pointing to the right on "Check-In," "Sports Stadium" and "Concessions" signs. Draw arrows pointing to the left on other signs. Tape, staple or nail signs to pole.

Barbell

Purchase or cut six Styrofoam disks that are 12 inches (30.5 cm) in diameter. Cut a hole in the center of each Styrofoam disk to fit over the end of a shower-curtain rod. Take the stopper off either end of shower-curtain rod. On each end wrap a rubber band several times to be an inside stopper and slide on three Styrofoam disks. Place stoppers on ends of rod again. Use acrylic paints and paint black.

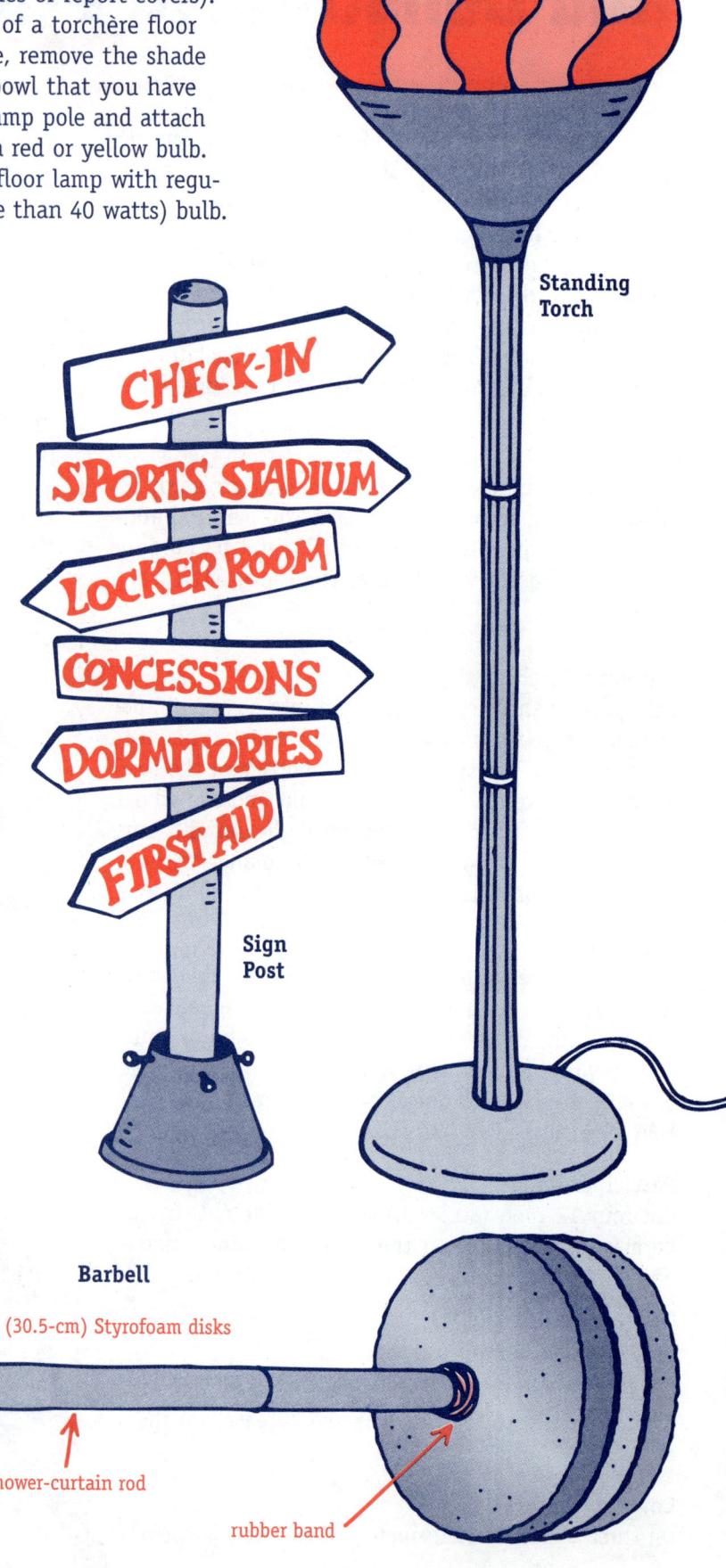

Standing Torch — transparent flames

Sign Post

Barbell — 12-inch (30.5-cm) Styrofoam disks, shower-curtain rod, stopper, rubber band

Stage Setup

The Stadium Backdrop, Sign Post and Standing Torch are used with various other elements to suggest the different locations for the skits: The Welcome Center, the Practice Arena, the arena for the Weight-Lifting Finals, the stadium for the 800-Meter Race and the arena for the Gymnastics final event. (See pp. 9-10 for instructions on constructing the necessary props.) Place Sign Post at upstage right and Standing Torch at upstage left. A bench is used in all but the first skit.

Skit 1

On a large sheet of butcher paper, print the phrase "Welcome, Athletes!" and staple, tape or tack to backdrop at stage right.

Skit 2

Remove Welcome, Athletes! sign. On a large sheet of butcher paper, print the phrase "Practice Arena" and staple, tape or tack to backdrop at stage right. Place bench at upstage center.

Skit 3

Remove Practice Arena sign and move bench to stage right. Onto a large sheet of butcher paper, print the phrase "Weight-Lifting Finals" and staple, tape or tack to backdrop at stage right. Place Barbell at center stage.

Skit 4

Remove Weight-Lifting Finals sign. On a large sheet of butcher paper, print the phrase "800-Meter Race" and staple, tape or tack to backdrop at stage right. Make a Start/Finish line by making a masking-tape line on floor at center stage.

Skit 5

Remove 800-Meter Race sign and Start/Finish masking-tape line. On a large sheet of butcher paper, print "Gymnastics" and staple, tape or tack to backdrop at stage right. Tape a different Country Placard to the front of the table in front of each chair.

NOTE: For skit 5, eliminate table and use chairs and clipboards for judges if space is limited.

© 2004 Gospel Light. Permission to photocopy granted. SonGames 2004 *Assemblies and Skits Production Guide*

Stadium Backdrop Pattern

14

© 2004 Gospel Light. Permission to photocopy granted. SonGames 2004 Assemblies and Skits Production Guide

SonGames 2004

John 3:16

Go Team!

VBSN·TV
OFFICIAL NETWORK OF
SonGames 2004

Props

For each skit, you will need the Stadium Backdrop (see p. 14) and the appropriate costume for each character (see pp. 7-8). Each individual skit also calls for the following props. Most of these items are household items, and all props should be gathered well ahead of time. Publish a list of needed items in your church bulletin. If some items can't be located, modify the skit to use something else.

Skit 1
- three large black suitcases or bags
- other miscellaneous luggage
- newspaper
- pink tutu or tights
- large adhesive label
- drink can
- marker
- cell phone
- microphone
- cosmetic powder puff
- empty squirt bottle

Skit 2
- Folded Letter (see p. 9)
- dumbbells and other small weights
- large sheet of brown paper
- resealable plastic bag with several cookies
- cell-phone charger
- tape
- pink stuffed pig
- large black suitcase or bag
- gymnastics ribbon (see p. 7)
- handkerchief
- dark eye shadow
- microphone
- cosmetic powder puff
- empty squirt bottle

Skit 3
- gymnastics ribbon (see p. 7)
- flowers
- pom-poms
- other gymnastic props (additional ribbons and pom-poms, balls, hoops, etc.)
- sports bag
- large gold medal
- cell phone
- microphone
- cosmetic powder puff
- empty squirt bottle

Skit 4
- Participant Tags (see p. 9)
- elastic or athletic bandage
- large adhesive label
- cold cream jar
- marker
- sports bag
- pins
- microphone

Skit 5
- Sessions 1-5 Motto Pennants or reproductions (see p. 4)
- Runner's Torch (see p. 9)
- Flip Sign (see p. 9)
- Scorecards (see p. 9)
- "ER" Patches (see p. 9)
- sheets of white paper
- markers
- large cardboard box (as for a microwave, television or other medium-sized appliance)
- rolled-up paper scroll
- inflatable globe ball
- gift package with "Thank you" printed on it in large letters
- white cloth (tablecloth, twin-sized bedsheet, three yards of fabric, etc.)
- bicycle with training wheels
- handkerchief
- tape, pins or needle and thread
- microphone
- cosmetic powder puff
- empty squirt bottle

Motto Pennants

SESSION 1

OPENING ASSEMBLY/SKIT

(10-15 minutes)

Materials: Bible with marker at Psalm 100:3, *SonGames* songbook and CD, CD player, word chart for songs "Join In!" and "The Lord Is God," Session 1 Motto Pennant or poster-board reproduction (see "Opening and Closing Assemblies," p. 4), Runner's Torch (see p. 9), costumes for characters (see pp. 7-8), items for stage setup (see p. 11), props (see p. 15).

Preparation: Set stage as directed in "Stage Setup" (see p. 11). Pack one large black suitcase or bag with crumpled newspaper and hand to Stella. Pack pink tutu or tights inside another large black suitcase or bag and hand to Brutus. Place label on drink can and print "Power Drink" on label. Pack third large black suitcase or bag with Power Drink can and crumpled newspaper; hand to Tumbelina. Pack other miscellaneous luggage with crumpled newspaper and place offstage right for Brutus, Stella and Tumbelina to carry on with large black bags when they enter. Give cell phone to Brutus who puts it in a pocket. Give microphone, cosmetic powder puff and empty squirt bottle to Stagehand.

Play songs from CD as children gather.

Welcome/Song

Welcome to the SonGames! Have you ever wondered what it might feel like to win a gold medal or to be on a winning Olympic team? You can be a part of our team by joining us every (day this week). You won't want to miss a moment of the action, especially since all of the action will help us learn how to join the greatest team of all—God's team!

At the Olympics that are being held in Athens, Greece, this year, the games begin when a huge torch is lit. Today, the SonGames will officially **begin with the lighting of our torch.** Play "SonGames 2004 Fanfare" from *SonGames* CD as a volunteer carries Runner's Torch from the back of the assembly hall to the Standing Torch at the front. Volunteer appears to light the Standing Torch by holding the Runner's Torch to the Standing Torch as someone offstage plugs in the lamp. **Let the SonGames begin!**

Lead children to sing "Join In!" **Now let's go to** the Welcome Station of the SonGames. The athletes are still arriving.

Cue *SonGames* CD sound effects to Bus.

Skit Script

(*Joe Gabbyola and Stagehand enter from left. Joe adjusts tie and clears his throat, as Stagehand powders Joe's nose with powder puff and pretends to spray him with hairspray from empty squirt bottle. Joe grimaces.*)

Director: (*Offstage.*) We're live in 5 . . . 4 . . . 3 . . . (*Stagehand gives Joe microphone and exits left carrying powder puff and squirt bottle.*) 2 . . . 1!

Joe: (*Joe speaks into microphone, facing audience as if facing a camera.*) Good afternoon, sports fans! I'm Joe Gabbyola. Welcome to VBSN's live coverage of the SonGames! It's going to be an exciting week as teams from all over the world come together in the spirit of sportsmanship. We're here just outside the beautiful SonGames Sports Stadium along with thousands of spectators waving signs of welcome to the athletes. (*Joe gestures toward the backdrop.*)

Right now we're awaiting the arrival of the team from the tiny country of Smallvania. This is the first time Smallvania will be competing in the SonGames and we will bring you live reports all week—the story behind each story. All the other teams have arrived, and Team Smallvania should arrive at any moment. (*With concern.*) Actually, they should be here by now. (*Joe looks at his watch and then offstage, pacing nervously back and forth.*) I'm sorry for the delay, but the Smallvanian team is really running late. I'm beginning to wonder if they're going to make it at all. (*Play sound effect Bus. Joe looks offstage right.*) Wait a minute. I see a bus coming now. (*Stella Swift, Tumbelina Turnover and Brutus Liftsalot enter from the back of the auditorium. They each carry a large black suitcase as well as other pieces of luggage. Brutus and Stella ad-lib arguing with each other as Tumbelina chatters excitedly. When they reach the stage, they place their bags upstage. The acronym H.E.L.P. U.S. is seen printed on their uniforms. Brutus stumbles over the bag he put down.*)

Stella: Hey, Brutus, watch it! (*Points finger at him.*) My power drink is in that bag. (*Shakes head in disgust.*) How'd I get stuck with a couple of amateur athletes like you two?

Brutus: Because the games are FOR amateur athletes! (*Brutus picks up bag and holds it close.*) Besides, this is MY bag. I have a big black one.

Stella: (*Tries to take bag.*) They're ALL black. It's mine. Now get your big Brutus hands off of it!

Brutus: If they're all black, how do you know this bag is yours? (*Stella and Brutus struggle over the bag. Tumbelina opens bag she carried and holds up a can with Power Drink label.*)

Tumbelina: Stella, here's your power drink and your bag. Now come on, you two, you've been arguing for the past three days! (*Stella retrieves can and bag from Tumbelina, putting the can back in bag.*)

Brutus: (*Crossing arms over chest.*) It's not my fault, Tumbelina. Stella keeps bugging me!

Stella: HA! Brutus, everything's your fault! We missed our flight here because YOU had to go back to the farm and milk YOUR precious cows one more time! Instead of a short plane trip, we had to take a three-day bus ride!

Brutus: That was not MY fault. My family needed me. The cows were depending on me!

Stella: Well, I'm not going to depend on you for anything more than trouble. My muscles are unbelievably stiff from that long bus ride. But I'm not going to lose MY races because of YOUR cows! (*Stella arches and rubs the small of her back, trying to stretch out.*)

Tumbelina: Aw, come on, Stella. You're using up all your energy complaining. Now that we're here at the SonGames, we all need to join in together as a team. (*She jumps up and down and claps her hands excitedly.*)

Stella: Tumbelina, who told you I needed a team? I'm a track athlete and I run ALONE. Which reminds me—I still have some training to do today. If you two expect to win anything, I'd suggest you get to work, too! And I don't mean milking cows!

Joe: (*Approaches them enthusiastically.*) Welcome, Team Smallvania! I'm Joe Gabbyola live on VBSN. (*Walks over to Stella, but speaks facing audience as if facing a camera. Stella ignores him and begins stretching and warming up.*) Stella Swift is Smallvania's best prospect for a gold medal. She's a world-class athlete who is the strong favorite to win the 200-, 400- and 800-meter races. Stella, our audience would love to hear your thoughts on—

Stella: (*Interrupting.*) Are you kidding? I've got to get totally focused here. I've worked and trained too hard to get sidetracked by the media. Do you know what the name "Stella" means in Greek? "Star." (*Draws a star in the air with her fingers.*) I'm here to perform like one. If you want to talk to Tinkerbell . . . (*Points with her thumb at Tumbelina.*)

Tumbelina: (*Helpfully.*) My name is pronounced tuhm-beh-LEE-nuh.

Stella: Yeah, yeah, whatever. If you want to talk to HER or Bruiser—

Brutus: (*Irritated.*) I'm Brutus!

Stella: (*Offhandedly.*) Whatever! (*To Joe.*) Talk with them if you want, but I'm not interested in any interviews. I have to run—and I mean REALLY RUN. (*Stella runs offstage right.*)

Joe: (*Moving on to Tumbelina who waves and smiles at the audience as if looking at a camera.*) Tumbelina Turnover is competing in the newest sporting event, freestyle gymnastics. How about it Tumbelina? Will you answer a few questions?

Tumbelina: Maybe one or two, but then I need to check in to my room.

Joe: The first thing I've got to ask is . . . (*He notices Brutus who has moved upstage and can be seen between Tumbelina and Joe, waving at the camera, flexing his muscles and mouthing "Hi, Mom!" Joe points to the letters on Brutus's uniform.*) about your team uniforms. Why do they say, "Help us"? (*Points microphone at Tumbelina.*)

Tumbelina: (*Giggles.*) They don't say "Help us"! The letters stand for our team motto. (*Using the logo on Brutus's uniform, she points to each letter as she explains.*) "Hope, Endurance, Loyalty and Peace—United Smallvania." (*She jumps up and down and cheers.*) YEA!

Brutus: (*Grins broadly.*) Tumbelina designed our uniforms. She is very artistic!

Tumbelina: Thanks, Brutus! That's really sweet of you. (*Brutus shuffles his feet in pleased embarrassment.*) Now, Mr. Gabbyola, why don't you ask Brutus some questions?

Joe: Thank you, Tumbelina!

Tumbelina: You're welcome! (*As* Joe *interviews* Brutus, Tumbelina *curtsies, grabs a few bags and skips offstage right.*)

Joe: (*To audience.*) Brutus Liftsalot has never competed at this level, but he looks strong in the weight-lifting competition. (Brutus *makes fists and flexes muscles to show strength.*) He works on his family's farm and is said to be a natural at weight lifting. (*To Brutus.*) Now tell us about your team. (Joe *points microphone at* Brutus.)

Brutus: (*Leaning toward microphone and speaking very slowly, clearly and a bit too loudly.*) Hello. First of all, I want to say we are VERY excited to be here competing. (Brutus *steps back and beams proudly, waves and mouths "Hi, Mom!"*)

Joe: I didn't see any coaches get off the bus with you. Are they coming later?

Brutus: (Brutus *leans into the microphone again. Each time he says "small," he brings his hands closer together.*) Well, you know, small country, small team, small budget. We call our coaches to get advice and instructions. (Brutus *pulls a cell phone out of his pocket to show* Joe.)

Joe: (*Looks at the audience and raises his eyebrows.*) Uh, huh. That's certainly unusual. (*To Brutus.*) Okay. Now about your training. Do you have any special equipment or strategy that gives you an edge over the competition?

Brutus: (Brutus *nods his head knowingly.*) Yes. I have a special set of weights that I take with me wherever I go. (Brutus *puts his arms up in a show of strength.*) But there is something else that will help me keep strong.

Joe: What is that?

Brutus: It's something that will help me stay focused here at the SonGames—especially since I've never been away from the farm. I'll give you a hint—it's pink!

Joe: Pink? Well, you've certainly got me curious!

Brutus: I'll show you! Give me a minute to find it. (Brutus *opens black bag, rummages around, pulls out a pink tutu and holds it up smiling broadly. Then realizing his mistake, he shoves it back into bag, embarrassed.*)

Joe: (*Laughing.*) Was that a tutu?

Brutus: (*Stammering, embarrassed.*) I must have gotten Tumbelina's bag by mistake. I was looking for my pink stuffed pig.

Joe: What does a pink stuffed pig have to do with weight lifting?

Brutus: When I was just a little weight lifter, my mama gave me this stuffed pig. I called him Suey, because that's the word you use to call a pig. Suey helps me get a good night's sleep, and if I get a good night's sleep, I can lift anything! (Brutus *begins flexing his muscles again.* Tumbelina *and* Stella *enter.* Tumbelina *carries a large black suitcase.*)

Tumbelina: (*Taps* Brutus *on the shoulder.*) Excuse me for interrupting, but, Brutus, I think you might have my bag. (Brutus *winks and nods at* Joe *before exchanging bags with* Tumbelina.) By the way, I talked Stella into getting a snack. You wanna come, Brutus? If we're going to join in as a team this week, we'd better start getting along. You and Stella can start by forgiving each other for all the fighting you did on the bus ride.

Stella: Hey, wait a minute! I'm coming because I'm hungry. I didn't say anything about joining your so-called team!

Tumbelina: But we ARE a team! We're Team Smallvania! (Tumbelina *twirls around and then strikes a dramatic pose with her arms curved over her head to the left and her right leg bent up at the knee.* Brutus *and* Stella *stare at her, dumbfounded.* Tumbelina *wobbles a bit but holds the pose.*)

Stella: (*After a moment.*) What is THAT supposed to be?

Tumbelina: (*Breaking pose.*) It's an *S*, of course—for Team Smallvania! This is my *S*-team pose! (*She twirls and strikes the pose once again.*)

Brutus: (*Shakes his head as if to clear it.*) Okay. Let's go eat. I'll even try to be nice to Stella. (Tumbelina *breaks pose to bounce up and down, clapping.*)

Stella: (*Sarcastically.*) Gee, thanks, big guy.

Tumbelina: Great! (Tumbelina *is bouncing with energy.*) I'm really starting to get excited! The dormitory is really nice, and they have a big practice arena and . . . (Tumbelina *skips and jumps up and down excitedly as she chatters to* Brutus *as they walk off, stage left.* Stella *follows rolling her eyes.*)

Joe: (*Moves to center stage and speaks as if into camera.*) Well, folks there you have it. Team Smallvania is joining in with enthusiasm here at the start of the SonGames. Will a good night's sleep and a hot meal help them focus and stay on course to victory? Tune in tomorrow for more live action from VBSN and your host, Joe Gabbyola! So long!

Director: (*Offstage.*) All right, that's it for today; that's a wrap. (*Joe hands microphone to Stagehand who enters from stage left.*)

Joe: (*To Stagehand.*) Man, I'm getting a little hungry myself! (*Both exit stage left.*)

Summary

Did you notice that the athletes from Smallvania are very different from each other? What kind of athlete is Brutus? (Weight lifter.) **Tumbelina?** (Gymnast.) **Stella?** (Runner.) **Even though they compete in different sports, they are still a team because their country chose them to represent Smallvania at the SonGames. This (week) at VBS you will get to be on a team, too. And you'll learn about being on the best team of all—God's team!**

Give a volunteer Session 1 Motto Pennant or reproduction to hold up. **Each (day) at the SonGames, we'll have a motto to help us remember what we're learning about being on God's team. The official Olympic motto is "Faster, Higher, Stronger." Today, what is our official SonGames motto?** ("Join In!")

Bible Memory Verse

God wants us to be on His team; and His Word, the Bible, tells us why. Open Bible and read Psalm 100:3. **We are God's people and He loves us. Today we'll talk about the good things that God gives us when we join His team of people who love Him.**

Prayer

Let's thank God for His love and forgiveness. Dear God, the Bible tells us that we are Your people. Thank You for loving us and sending Jesus so that we can become members of Your team. In Jesus' name, amen.

Song

Sing "The Lord Is God."

Announcements/Dismissal

Explain procedure for Session 1 and dismiss children to classes.

CLOSING ASSEMBLY

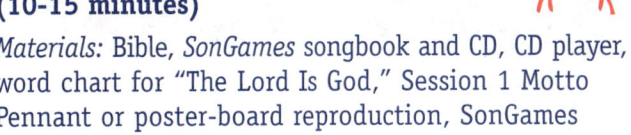

(10-15 minutes)

Materials: Bible, *SonGames* songbook and CD, CD player, word chart for "The Lord Is God," Session 1 Motto Pennant or poster-board reproduction, SonGames Medals (see p. 4).

Play songs from CD as children gather. Give Session 1 Motto Pennant or reproduction to a volunteer to hold up during assembly.

Song

Sing "The Lord Is God" from *SonGames* cassette/CD.

Prizes

Distribute SonGames Medals and/or other prizes (for more information, see p. 4).

Review

I'm glad you were here today at the SonGames! What is today's motto? ("Join In!") Have volunteer show Session 1 Motto Pennant or reproduction. **In our Bible story today, who joined God's team and believed Jesus is God's Son?** (Saul, or Paul.) **God wants all of us on His team, too. Let's say our verse together.** Recite Psalm 100:3 aloud together.

TIP: Select a student to say the verse aloud before all students recite it together. Each session, select a different student to say the verse.

Prayer

Dear God, thank You for sending Your Son, Jesus, to show us how we can join God's team. Thank You for forgiving us and loving us. In Jesus' name, amen.

Announcements/Dismissal

Make announcements and invite children back for the next session. **Come back (tomorrow) for more fun with all your friends at the SonGames. We'll hear what happens when Paul meets other members of God's team!**

SESSION 2

OPENING ASSEMBLY/SKIT

(10-15 minutes)

Materials: Bible with marker at Hebrews 10:24, *SonGames* songbook and CD, CD player, word charts for songs "Join In!" and "Teamwork," Sessions 1 and 2 Motto Pennants or poster-board reproductions (see "Opening and Closing Assemblies," p. 4), costumes for characters (see pp. 7-8), items for stage setup (see p. 12), props (see p. 15).

Preparation: Set stage as directed in "Stage Setup" (see p. 12). Place dumbbells and other small weights beside bench at upstage center. In large sheet of brown paper, place resealable plastic bag with several cookies, Folded Letter and cell-phone charger; wrap to form a package and tape to secure. Pack pink stuffed pig and brown paper package in large black bag. Place black bag upstage left. Give Tumbelina gymnastics ribbon and handkerchief to tuck into her waistband. Using dark eye shadow, create shadows under Brutus's eyes. Give microphone, cosmetic powder puff and empty squirt bottle to Stagehand.

Play songs from CD as children gather.

Welcome/Song

Lead children to sing "Join In!" **Welcome back to the SonGames! Yesterday we met athletes from the country of Smallvania—Tumbelina, Brutus and Stella. Stella didn't want to . . .** Hold up or point to Session 1 Motto Pennant or reproduction as students yell out "Join In!" **with her teammates. But let's see how Team Smallvania is doing today after they've all had a good night's sleep.**

Cue *SonGames* CD sound effects to Horn.

Skit Script

(*Joe enters weight-lifting arena, with Stagehand adjusting Joe's tie, applying more powder, etc.*)

Director: (*Offstage.*) We're live in 5 . . . 4 . . . 3 . . . (*Joe grabs microphone from Stagehand who exits offstage carrying powder puff and squirt bottle.*) 2 . . . 1!

Joe: (*Facing audience as if looking at a camera.*) Buenos días [BWEH-nohs DEE-uhs]! That's Spanish for "Good day!" I'm Joe Gabbyola, and this is a GOOD day to be here at the beautiful SonGames Sports Stadium! We're continuing with VBSN's coverage of spectacular sporting events.

(*Optional: Show video highlights [see p. 4 for more information].*)

Joe: Here at VBSN we're giving you personal and exclusive coverage of team Smallvania. (*As Joe speaks, Brutus enters and crosses upstage, beginning to warm up. He struggles to lift a small weight, tries again, grimaces, wipes his brow and shakes his head in disbelief. He paces back and forth, appearing to give himself a pep talk. Pantomime continues during Joe's report.*) If you watched yesterday's broadcast, you know this team has had a rough start. (*Brutus continues practicing but also listens to Joe and responds appropriately.*) Will this tiny group be able to pull together as a team? (*Brutus nods his head.*) They have only one day of practice before the real competitions begin. I don't know if they've got what it takes to do it. (*Brutus sadly shakes his head.*) The H.E.L.P. U.S. on their uniforms looks more like a cry for help than a team logo. (*Joe laughs a little; Brutus looks at the letters, slumps his shoulders and looks defeated.*) Because their coaches are back in Smallvania, the only coaching they'll receive here at the games will be by cell phone. (*Brutus picks up cell phone, pushes buttons and shakes phone; then giving up, he shrugs his shoulders and puts it down, shaking his head sadly.*)

Of course they could score big points in track and field with their star athlete, Stella Swift. (*Brutus hears this and tries to put on a show of strength by lifting his weights, but he's still struggling.*) But odds are against them in both weight lifting and the new event of freestyle gymnastics. (*Brutus drops his weights and looking down, shakes his head and begins to pace back and forth.*) Now we've even heard reports that one of their athletes might be sick. (*Brutus abruptly stops his pacing and sadly mouths "Me."*)

© 2004 Gospel Light. Permission to photocopy granted. SonGames 2004 *Assemblies and Skits Production Guide*

Brutus: (*Brutus pulls out cell phone and dials.*) Coach? Coach? Can you hear me? (*Takes a few steps and then puts it up to his ear again.*) Can you hear me now? Coach, are you there? ARGH! The battery's dead and I can't find my charger!

Joe: (*Turning to Brutus.*) Here's Brutus Liftsalot, the farmer turned champion weight lifter. Let's see if we can get a quick comment from him. (*To Brutus.*) Good morning, Brutus. Do you think you're going to win in the weight-lifting competition?

Brutus: (*Distracted.*) When I got off the bus yesterday, I thought I COULD win, but now I'm not so sure. I've had a few . . . complications.

Joe: (*Smiles and speaks toward the audience [camera].*) What would those be? (*Points microphone at Brutus without looking at him, still smiling and looking front as if into camera.*)

Brutus: (*Tired and defeated. As he speaks, we hear his desperation and sorrow grow.*) My special weights and barbell are lost! Remember my stuffed pig, Suey? Well, I can't find Suey anywhere. I didn't sleep a wink last night! Now I'm feeling a little . . . well, . . . homesick! I haven't felt like eating. I can barely even lift these small practice weights. I can't call my coach and . . . and . . . and . . . (*Brutus crosses his arms over his chest and sticks out his lower lip as he struggles not to cry.*)

Joe: Hey, come on there, Brutus! Never give up! (*Brutus hangs his head and shakes it. Joe shakes his head and sighs.*) Well, folks, there you have it. Equipment problems and other difficulties often occur at these events. That's when athletes really need their teams to encourage them and help them through the rough spots. Unless Brutus's fellow athletes from Smallvania can manage to overcome their differences and help him out, he may be finished before he starts! (*Brutus looks up as if Joe's words have given him an idea.*) For VBSN, this is Joe Gabbyola. Join us again for more live coverage of the SonGames. (*Stagehand enters from left. Joe hands microphone to Stagehand as they walk off, stage left. Stella enters from right, jogging across stage.*)

Stella: Hey ya, Brutus. (*She exits left.*)

Brutus: (*Calling and waving.*) Stella! STELLA!

(*Stella jogs backward to stand next to Brutus, looks at her watch and then jogs in place impatiently.*)

Brutus: Stella, do you have a minute? I need to talk to someone.

Stella: (*Jogging in place.*) You've got ten seconds.

Brutus: Well, it's like this. You see, . . . I'm having problems—

Stella: (*Stella cuts him off.*) Oops, time's up! (*Stella jogs off, stage left. Brutus lifts his hand as if to stop her and then drops his hand in discouragement, sighs and turns back to his weights. Tumbelina enters from right, smiling, skipping, whistling, and twirling gymnastics ribbon. She stops abruptly when she sees Brutus.*)

Tumbelina: (*Kind and concerned.*) Hey, Brutus. You don't look so good.

Brutus: Oh, you don't want to hear about my problems. (*Sadly, he shakes his head and waves her off.*)

Tumbelina: Of course I do. What's a teammate for? We're supposed to encourage each another. We're Team Smallvania! (*She twirls and strikes the S-team pose—arms curved over head to the left with right leg bent at knee.*) Maybe it would help if you told me what's bothering you.

Brutus: (*As he speaks, Brutus gets more and more emotional until he breaks down completely.*) Well, this is kind of embarrassing, . . . (*He shuffles his feet.*) but I've never slept away from home before. I opened my suitcase to get Suey—he's my stuffed pig—but he wasn't there! I think he got left behind on the bus. Without Suey, I couldn't fall asleep. I tossed and turned all night long. This morning, I missed my family so much that I just felt sick. My special weight-lifting equipment got left on the bus, and when I try to lift these borrowed weights, I can't lift even the smallest one. (*Demonstrates by trying to lift a small weight but failing.*) I'm WEAK! I tried to call my coach, but my cell phone is dead. (*He sniffles loudly.*) And Joe Gabbyola just announced to the whole world on TV that I'm a LOSER! (*Brutus sits down on the bench with a thud, burying his face in his hands.*)

Tumbelina: There, there. (*Tumbelina pats him on the shoulder and hands him the handkerchief.*) Blow. (*Brutus blows his nose in an overly dramatic way. Play sound effect Horn.*)

Brutus: I'm just soooo sad! (*Breaks down again and cries into handkerchief.*)

Tumbelina: Cheer up, Brutus! I've got a surprise for you! Last night I realized one of my bags was missing. So I went to the bus station to pick it up. Your bag was there, too! (*She points to big black bag in the upstage left corner of the stage. Brutus is overjoyed.*) I put it there earlier. I thought you'd see it when you came to work out. (*Tumbelina skips over to bag, effortlessly picks it up, carries it to the surprised Brutus and sets it down.*)

Brutus: Thanks, Tumbelina! (*He tries to pick up bag but can't. Shocked and embarrassed, he tries again, but the bag doesn't budge.*) I'm a wreck! I'm so tired and weak, I can't pull my own weight around here! (*Sits down and cries into handkerchief.*)

Tumbelina: (*Thoughtfully.*) Brutus, last night at the cafeteria, all you had was a glass of milk. Have you eaten anything today?

Brutus: No, not really. (*He sniffles.*) I went to the cafeteria, but nothing looked good. It just made me miss my mom's cooking. (*Wistfully.*) She makes the best snufflejoodles. (*Starts to cry again.*)

Tumbelina: Brutus, on the three-day bus ride over here, all you ate was junk food! I think you just need something good to eat and a little nap. You'll feel better in no time. (*Reaching in bag, she pulls out Suey and hands it to Brutus. He smiles and hugs it close. Then, embarrassed, he puts the stuffed pig on the bench next to him.*) Here. This package arrived today. I think it's from your family. (*Tumbelina pulls package out of bag and hands to Brutus.*)

Brutus: (*Slowly smiles broadly. Rips open package.*) It is! Oh, look! It's my mother's snufflejoodles! (*Brutus takes a cookie out of bag and takes a big bite.*) MMmmmmm! (*Smiles in satisfaction. Pulls out Folded Letter from package, glances at it, starts to sniffle and hands it to Tumbelina.*) Can you read it for me, Tumbelina?

Tumbelina: Sure, Brutus. (*Opens the letter, unfolding and unfolding it several times until it is full size. Brutus stands and helps her hold it, so the audience can read it.*) "Dear Brutus, We are so proud of you! We know you will do your best. We love you. Your Family. P.S. Here is your cell-phone charger. You left it in the barn."

(*Brutus finds cell-phone charger in the package, holds it up happily and then bursts into tears.*)

Tumbelina: What's the matter now, Brutus?

Brutus: Nothing. (*Holds handkerchief up to his eyes and sniffles loudly.*) I'm just sooooo happy! (*Brutus blows his nose. Play sound effect Horn.*)

(*Tumbelina chuckles as Brutus effortlessly picks up his bag of weights. They exit together stage right.*)

Summary

Which teammate helped Brutus when he was sad and discouraged? (Tumbelina.) **Which teammate did NOT help Brutus?** (Stella.) **Tumbelina helped Brutus by encouraging him and cheering him up when he was sad and upset. Who else encouraged Brutus by sending him a BIG letter?** (His family.) **They sent him a package and a letter to show him they loved him. We can do loving and encouraging things for other people, too!** Give volunteer Session 2 Motto Pennant or reproduction to hold up. **What is today's official motto?** ("Team Up!") **We'll learn ways to help each other do our best and ways to do good things for others, too.**

Bible Memory Verse

Let's read what the Bible says about encouragement. Open Bible and read Hebrews 10:24 aloud. **To "spur one another on" means to encourage or cheer each other. We can encourage each other to be more loving and do good things. God helps and encourages us, too! One way God helped us was by sending Jesus to make a way for us to become members of God's team.**

Prayer

Dear God, thank You for giving us friends to help and encourage us. Please help us to encourage others, too. In Jesus' name, amen.

Song

Sing "Teamwork."

Announcements/Dismissal

Explain procedure for Session 2 and dismiss children to classes.

CLOSING ASSEMBLY

(10-15 minutes)

Materials: Bible, *SonGames* songbook and CD, CD player, word chart for "Teamwork," Session 2 Motto Pennant or poster-board reproduction, SonGames Medals (see p. 4).

Play songs from CD as children gather. Give Session 2 Motto Pennant or reproduction to a volunteer to hold up during assembly.

Song

Sing "Teamwork" from *SonGames* cassette/CD.

Prizes

Distribute SonGames Medals and/or other prizes (for more information, see p. 4).

Review

In today's Bible story, Paul was helped by his friends in Damascus and by Barnabas in Jerusalem. Choose a class to stand and recite Hebrews 10:24 aloud. **Today you learned what it means to "spur one another on." What is a word we can use for "spur[ring] one another on"?** ("Encourage." "Cheer.") **Encouraging someone is like cheering others on. That reminds me of today's motto! Let's say it as a cheer!** Have volunteer show Session 2 Motto Pennant or reproduction. **What is today's official motto?** Kids shout "Team Up!" **An important thing that we can do as a team is to cheer each other on to do good things and to help others.**

Prayer

Dear God, we've had a great time today learning what it means to team up. Please help us be loving and kind. Please help us encourage others, too. Thank You for sending Your Son, Jesus, so that we can be members of Your team. In Jesus' name, amen.

Announcements/Dismissal

Make announcements and invite children back for the next session. **Come back (tomorrow) to hear about something everyone competing in a sport wants to do—"Get Strong!"**

SESSION 3

OPENING ASSEMBLY/SKIT

(10-15 minutes)

Materials: Bible with marker at Psalm 119:28,32. *SonGames* songbook and CD, CD player, word charts for songs "Join In!" and "Get Strong," Sessions 1-3 Motto Pennants or poster-board reproductions (see "Opening and Closing Assemblies," p. 4), costumes for characters (see pp. 7-8), items for stage setup (see p. 12), props (see p. 15).

Preparation: Set stage as directed in "Stage Setup" (see p. 12). Pack gymnastics ribbon, flowers, pom-poms and other gymnastic props in sports bag and give to Tumbelina. Stella wears large gold medal around her neck. Give cell phone to Brutus. Give microphone, cosmetic powder puff and empty squirt bottle to Stagehand.

Play songs from CD as children gather.

Welcome/Song

Lead children to sing "Join In!" **Welcome back to the SonGames! So far, we've learned that members of God's team . . .** Hold up or point to Session 1 Motto Pennant or reproduction as students yell "Join In!" and then hold up or point to Session 2 Motto Pennant or reproduction as students yell "Team Up!" **We know that God gives us love and forgiveness when we join His team. We've also seen how important it is to encourage and help one another. Yesterday we saw how much Brutus needed someone to encourage him. Today is the big day of his weight-lifting competition. Let's see how Brutus does!**

Cue *SonGames* CD sound effects to Cheering Crowd.

Skit Script

Brutus: (*Brutus enters from stage right, talking on cell phone and crossing to upstage center.*) Okay, Coach. I will, Coach. Thank you, Coach. Goodbye. (*Brutus puts phone down, begins stretching and flexing his muscles and then starts lifting weights.*)

(*Joe and Stagehand enter and cross to downstage center. Stagehand preps Joe as usual; Joe is annoyed, grabs his microphone and shoos Stagehand away. Stagehand gathers props and exits left, hanging head and pouting.*)

Director: (*Offstage.*) We're live in 5 . . . 4 . . . 3 . . . 2 . . . 1! (*Joe's expression changes from annoyance to a huge grin.*)

Joe: (*Standing center stage and holding microphone.*) Jambo [JAHM-boh]! That's Swahili for "Hello!" I'm Joe Gabbyola and I hope you're having a good day like I'm having a good day providing for you VBSN's LIVE coverage of the SonGames.

(*Optional: Show video highlights [see p. 4 for more information].*)

Joe: Today we continue our exclusive coverage of the team from the tiny country of Smallvania. We are here at the weight-lifting event to watch Brutus Liftsalot in the finals. Competition started full throttle for this team just moments ago as Stella Swift, their star runner, ran on all cylinders to take first place in the 200-meter sprint. (*Joe motions offstage right for Stella to come forward. She enters.*) Here she is now, just moments after her big win! Stella, what can you tell us about your race today? (*He sticks microphone in her face.*)

Stella: (*Stella speaks a bit breathlessly.*) Well, Joe, everything went according to plan. I spoke to my coach earlier this morning and we went over all the basics. I approached the race with confidence, remembered my coach's words, ran steady and strong, and it paid off in victory. (*Stella raises her hands in triumph.*)

Joe: Stella, I think our viewers are aware that you (*Points at Stella.*) are the real star on this team, and today you really showed it. (*During the following dialogue, Joe gestures broadly with his hands. Stella has to back out of the way as he gets a bit too enthusiastic with his gestures.*) You were quick off the line, you went by the playbook, and you ran the extra yard. Do you think your teammates will be similarly successful as well?

Stella: (*Sarcastically.*) Ha! What do you think? (*Confidently.*) Look, I've got a really good chance of winning my next two races. But my teammates are from the minor leagues. Tinkerbell should stick to decorating T-shirts, and Brutus oughta be plowing the back forty on the family farm. I don't see any way they can be strong enough to win medals. The reason I'M a star runner is because I work at it and I obey everything my coach tells me to do.

Joe: What's next for you, Stella?

Stella: Well, tomorrow I race again, but for now I'm watching Brutus in the weight-lifting competition. Tumbelina insisted I meet her here. (*Tumbelina enters from stage right, carrying sports bag, smiles and waves to Stella and sits on bench at stage right.*) She seems to think it may help Brutus if we cheer him on. Whatever. I say a real champ doesn't need a bunch of squealing, screaming cheerleaders; but hey, I'm here, so I might as well watch, right?

Joe: Thanks for talking to us, Stella. Congratulations on your victory. (*Stella sits next to Tumbelina. Joe turns to audience as if speaking to the camera. During Joe's monologue, Brutus stretches, shakes his hands, cracks his neck, flexes his muscles and in other ways warms up. Tumbelina pantomimes clapping and cheering, speaking excitedly to Stella who rolls her eyes and seems impatient with them both.*) Alright sports fans, here's what we know so far about the weight-lifting competition: This is Brutus's final round, and he is solidly in fourth place. This last lift could literally leave him a legend! If he can pass his limit and land this last lift, he could leap into third place, winning the bronze medal! Brutus looks a lot stronger today than he did yesterday, but you've got to wonder what's left in him for this last lift. (*Brutus looks over at Joe in annoyance. Joe speaks in the classic sportscaster's whisper.*) All right . . . this is it . . . you can feel the electricity in the air. (*Brutus reaches up to feel the air and then shakes his head and shrugs his shoulders.*) This is gut-check time, folks. Is Brutus hungry enough to go all out here? (*Brutus glances down at his stomach, rubs it and shakes his head in agreement. He steps up to his weights.*) Brutus is stepping up to his weights like a batter to the plate. If he makes this lift, it's a home run! If he misses, he'll be sitting on the sidelines crying in his milk. (*With determination, Brutus bends, adjusts his grip, grimaces and very slowly lifts the weights to his thighs. He then lunges forward and thrusts the weights over his head and holds them there, shaking as if they are incredibly heavy. Play sound effect Cheering Crowd.*)

Joe: (*Excited.*) It might be . . . it could be . . . it is! Brutus Liftsalot has done it! He's just won the bronze medal! This is amazing, folks! You've just seen it live, right here on VBSN! Brutus Liftsalot has just taken the bronze medal in the SonGames weight-lifting competition! (*Brutus puts the weights down and walks the circumference of the stage with his arms raised in victory. He turns to wave at Tumbelina and Stella. They are jumping, cheering and even hugging each other. Then Stella composes herself and pulls away, straightening up. But she starts to smile and clap again as Joe crosses over to Brutus to interview him.*) What do you have to say to all your fans out there, Brutus? How does it feel to win the bronze medal? (*Shoves microphone in his face.*)

Brutus: Fans?! (*Shaking his head in disbelief.*) Oh, it feels great, Joe! I'd just like to thank my coach for all his good coaching and my family and friends who have been praying for me back home. Thank you all! (*Pumps fist in air.*) Go, Smallvania!

Joe: Brutus, I saw you were on the phone just before your last lift. Were you talking to your coach?

Brutus: Yes. He reminded me to follow my training routine and to ignore ALL distractions. (*Brutus turns slightly away from Joe and rolls his eyes and gestures slightly to indicate Joe as the distraction.*) He also told me to never give up! He also said he had a lot of confidence in me.

Joe: Can you tell us why he has so much confidence in you?

Brutus: Because I am a good listener and I always obey my coach! That helps make me strong. (*Brutus flexes his muscles.*) Well, that and a good night's sleep.

Joe: (*To audience as if to a camera.*) Well, folks, there you have it! The cow man has made the competition cower in fear! He milked this competition for every drop of victory! Join us tomorrow when Smallvania's star athlete, Stella Swift, makes a run for more gold in the 400- and 800-meter races. This is Joe Gabbyola for VBSN sports. Sooooo long, folks!

Director: (*Offstage.*) That's a wrap! (*Tumbelina runs up to Joe, hugs him, nearly knocking him over. Joe exits. Then she runs to Brutus, hugs him and then bounces up and down, clapping.*)

Stella: (*Stella walks over and shakes Brutus's hand formally.*) Congratulations, Brutus. (*Slaps him on the shoulder.*) You really surprised me. I didn't think you had a chance! (*Stella continues thoughtfully.*) Ya know . . . as crazy as it sounds . . . we might actually have a shot at all of us going home with medals. (*Points at Tumbelina.*) If by some miracle YOU should place in the top three! (*Tumbelina bounces up and down, giggling.*)

Tumbelina: (*Excitedly.*) I think I can do it, too! I need to practice my routine. Would you watch it and give me some helpful hints?

Brutus: Sure, Tumbelina. Like you said yesterday, we're a team. Team Smallvania! (*He awkwardly twirls around and strikes Tumbelina's S-team pose. Tumbelina bounces up and down, clapping in delight.*)

Stella: Before we get too excited here, let's see her routine.

Tumbelina: Alright! But let me tell you, I didn't like the routine my coach gave me, so I've made a few last-minute changes. It's a little rough. Since my coach isn't here, she'll never know.

Brutus: (*Interrupts Tumbelina.*) Tumbelina, I think it's a mistake not to listen to your coach.

Tumbelina: Oh, phooey, it'll be fine. Besides I'm an artist and I need to express myself! But first I need to take a deep breath (*Dramatically takes a deep breath.*) and FEEL the moment! (*Tumbelina tosses back her head, does a little twirl and raises her hand over her head with a flourish.*)

Stella: (*Skeptically.*) Let's just see your stuff, Tinkerbell. Then we'll know how the moment feels.

Tumbelina: Fine. (*Tumbelina strikes a dramatic pose and takes a gulping deep breath. She lunges into a sloppy, silly routine. She takes ribbons, scarves or pom-poms and flower petals out of her bag and tosses them in the air. She does bad cartwheels, somersaults, jumps, twirls and poses— all with dramatic facial expressions. Brutus and Stella look at each other dumbfounded and then grimace and shake their heads in disbelief. Tumbelina finishes with a balancing pose she has trouble holding and looks at her teammates expectantly, hoping for applause.*)

Brutus: (*Trying to be kind.*) Hmmm. There may be room for a little improvement here and there.

Stella: Room for improvement?! That was terrible! Why don't you just perform it in the dark? That way the judges won't see you! (*Tumbelina puts her hand on her heart dramatically and her lip quivers.*)

Brutus: Come on, Stella. (*Puts his hands on her shoulders.*) We're all on the same team here. How about we help Tumbelina, not insult her. Tumbelina, if you want your routine to be stronger, it'd be a good idea to listen to your coach. Let's call her and talk this over. Let's pray about it, too.

Stella: Now THAT makes sense. 'Cause she's going to need all the help she can get to make THAT routine look good! (*They exit left, with Brutus patting Tumbelina on the back.*)

Summary

Pause to allow volunteers to respond to the following questions: **Did Brutus listen to his coach? Did he do a good job in his competition? Did Tumbelina listen to her coach? Does she have a good routine for her competition? Sometimes it's hard for us to obey God's Word, but God has promised to help us when we ask.** Give volunteer Session 3 Motto Pennant or reproduction to hold up. **What is today's official motto?** ("Get Strong!") **We'll discover different ways God will help us get strong to obey His Word, the Bible.**

Bible Memory Verse

The Bible helps us to be strong as we follow and obey God. This is what we read in the Bible about obeying. Open Bible and read Psalm 119:28,32 aloud. **God's Word is the Bible and it gives us strength to obey Him. When we follow, or obey, God's commands, it is like practicing a sport or gymnastics routine. We get better and better. Doing what is right becomes easier.**

Prayer

Let's thank God for His help to obey. Dear God, thank You for giving us the Bible to help us obey.

And thank You for the other members of Your team who help us remember to do what is right. Help us as we practice obeying. In Jesus' name, amen.

Song

Sing "Get Strong."

Announcements/Dismissal

Explain procedure for Session 3 and dismiss children to classes.

CLOSING ASSEMBLY

(10-15 minutes)

Materials: Bible, *SonGames* songbook and CD, CD player, word chart for "Get Strong," Session 3 Motto Pennant or poster-board reproduction, SonGames Medals (see p. 4).

Play songs from CD as children gather. Give Session 3 Motto Pennant or reproduction to a volunteer to hold up during assembly.

Song

Sing "Get Strong" from *SonGames* cassette/CD.

Prizes

Distribute SonGames Medals and/or other prizes (for more information, see p. 4).

Review

In today's Bible story, Paul faced problems as he traveled. But Paul stayed strong and obeyed God. Paul received help from his friends. Who else helped Paul? (God.) **Today's verse tells us about ways that God can help us, too.** Choose a class to stand and recite Psalm 119:28,32. **God's commands are rules that help us know the best ways to live and the best things to do. If we practice following God's rules, we'll get better at doing them. But the best part is that God will HELP us get stronger if we ask Him!** Have volunteer show Session 3 Motto Pennant or reproduction. **"Get Strong!" reminds us that God will help us get strong and obey His commands.**

Prayer

Dear God, please help us to follow Your instructions. We love You and want to obey You. Thank You, God, for giving us love and helping us obey You. Thank You for sending Jesus so that we can become members of Your team. In Jesus' name, amen.

Announcements/Dismissal

Make announcements and invite children back for the next session. **Come back (tomorrow) for more fun with all your friends at the SonGames. We'll hear about some ways God can help us keep on, even when it's hard.**

SESSION 4

OPENING ASSEMBLY/SKIT

(10 to 15 minutes)

Materials: Bible with marker at Isaiah 41:10, SonGames songbook and CD, CD player, word charts for songs "Join In!" and "Do Not Be Afraid," Sessions 1-4 Pennants or poster-board reproductions (see "Opening and Closing Assemblies," p. 4), costumes for characters (see pp. 7-8), items for stage setup (see p. 13), props (see p. 15).

Preparation: Set stage as directed in "Stage Setup" (see p. 13). Wrap Stella's foot and ankle with elastic or athletic bandage. Place a large adhesive label on cold cream jar and print on label "C.H.A.M.P.S. Muscle Cream." Put jar in sports bag and give to Brutus. Pin a Participant Tag to each runner's back, including Stella's. Give microphone to Joe.

Play songs from CD as children gather.

Welcome/Song

Lead children to sing "Join In!" **Welcome back! It's another (day) of the SonGames. We've learned a lot this week about what it means to be on God's team.** As you say each of the mottoes that follow, pause, hold up or point to the appropriate Motto Pennant or reproduction and signal students to repeat them. **First we learned we need to "Join In!" Then we learned it's good to "Team Up!" Yesterday we learned that when it comes to obeying God's Word, it's important to "Get Strong!" We've seen the team of Smallvania discover these lessons, too. So far, Brutus and Stella have won medals in their competitions. But today Stella runs her last two races. Let's see what happens.**

Cue *SonGames* CD sound effects to Cheering Crowd.

Skit Script

Joe: (*Enters and faces audience as if speaking to a camera.*) Guten Tag [GOO-tehn TAHG], sports fans in Germany and around the world! I'm reporting live from the SonGames Sports Stadium where the 800-meter race will be starting soon. (*Optional: Show video highlights [see p. 4 for more information].*)

Joe: Let's review what's happened with the team from Smallvania. Yesterday, weight lifter Brutus Liftsalot surprised everyone by winning the bronze medal. Their star athlete, Stella Swift, also medaled when she took the gold in the 200-meter race. But there's bad news. (*Pauses dramatically.*) This morning as Stella ran the 400-meter race, she ran hard and fast. She was in the lead approaching the finish line when suddenly she fell . . . and fell HARD! (*Optional: Show video of Stella falling and then crawling to the finish line.*) Obviously injured, she crawled across the finish line and won the bronze! Doctors rushed to her aid. The last we saw Stella, she was being carried from the track on a stretcher. It's been several hours now and we're waiting to get a report on her condition before the next race starts. (*Looks offstage.*) It looks like they're coming out of the first-aid station now. (*Stella, Brutus, and Tumbelina enter from stage right. Stella's ankle is bandaged and she is limping.*)

Brutus: Now be careful, Stella.

Tumbelina: (*Encouraging.*) That's good, Stella. You're doing better! The doctor said your ankle is well enough to run the last race! (*They help Stella to the bench where she sits.*)

Stella: (*Discouraged.*) Well, maybe I could manage to jog around the track, but there's no way I can run fast enough to WIN! I'm out of the race!

Brutus: What do you mean? You can't just give up!

Stella: (*Determined.*) Well, I'm sure not going to make a fool of myself! People expect me to WIN. I don't want to run if I don't have a chance to get a medal.

Tumbelina: (*To Brutus, wringing her hands.*) Oh, dear! What are we going to do? We've got to think of something!

Brutus: Okay. Hmmmm . . . I'm thinking of something blue . . . it's round . . . and—

Tumbelina: (*Interrupts.*) That's not what I meant, Brutus!

Stella: (*Rolls her eyes.*) Oh, brother! We're not a team. We're a circus act! (*Brutus and Tumbelina both react in surprise.*)

Brutus: Did you say "team," Stella?

Stella: Oh, never mind. (*She waves off Brutus and rubs her ankle.*)

Tumbelina: (*Leaning down to look right in her face.*) You said "team," Stella! So now you're part of Team Smallvania? (*Tumbelina and Brutus both twirl and give the S-team pose.*)

Stella: Not exactly . . . but . . . (*She smiles a small smile.*) I guess we are starting to gel a little.

Tumbelina: (*Smiling broadly.*) I think the same thing!

Brutus: Back on the farm, my team of horses pulls together and helps each other keep on going when it's hard. We can pull together, too.

Stella: (*Rubs her ankle and speaks with discouragement in her voice.*) I don't think I want to keep on, Brutus.

(*During the following monologue, Brutus, Tumbelina and Stella pantomime talking together.*)

Joe: (*Steps to front of stage and speaks to audience as if to a camera.*) Wow! Talk about the thrill of victory and the agony of de feet! (*Points down to Stella's feet.*) Ha. Ha. Just a little joke there, folks. But seriously, this team is looking desperate. With Stella Swift injured, their chances of winning another medal are really falling off. I guess you could say Stella is a "falling star." Heh, heh. Uh, that's another joke, okay? Wait a minute. Let's see what they're talking about now.

Stella: (*Stubbornly.*) I just don't want to run a race I can't win!

Tumbelina: (*Pulls Brutus aside.*) We've just GOT to think of something that will help Stella run that race! I know she can do it. I'm afraid she'll feel worse if she doesn't even try!

Brutus: (*Slowly.*) I'm thinking . . . I'm thinking . . . I'm thinking of something I use on the farm—

Tumbelina: (*Scolding.*) Brutus! This is NOT the time to play games!

Brutus: (*Hastily.*) I'm thinking of my special muscle cream I use from home. It helps muscle sprains! (*Pulls jar from his bag. To Stella.*) Alright, Stella. Unwrap your ankle. (*Stella looks at him a bit skeptically but goes along and unwraps the bandage.*) This is just what you need to get back on track! (*Brutus laughs at his own joke. Stella holds her foot up to him.*)

Joe: (*To audience as if to a camera.*) This group is really showing teamwork. They can smell victory (*Sniffs air and makes a face.*) and it doesn't smell very good. Wait a minute—whew, what's that smell? (*Everyone starts holding their noses and fanning their hands in front of their faces.*)

Tumbelina: Stella, is that your feet that smell?!

Stella: (*Wrinkles nose.*) No, I don't know what that is. It smells like sour milk!

Brutus: More like sour cream! I call it C.H.A.M.P.S. (*Holds label of jar, so audience can see. Points to each letter in turn.*) Cows Help Athletes Mend Painful Sprains. It's a muscle cream we make back on the farm.

Stella: Whew, if it works, I guess I can stand the smell. Maybe it'll keep the other runners from getting too close to me!

Brutus: Oh, it works all right. (*Brutus finishes rubbing cream on her ankle.*) Now try a few exercises to see if it's helping. First, stretch out your ankle. (*Tumbelina helps Stella lift her leg up and down, as they try to follow Brutus's mixed-up directions.*) Stretch back, left, up and right . . . 1 . . . 2 . . . 3 . . . 4. Okay, now drop it DOWN a little higher . . . higher . . . no, put it UP a little lower. Okay, now lift it sideways a little to the left and stretch.

Stella: Do you really think this will work?

Brutus: Well, it can't hurt. But something even better is remembering that God can ALWAYS help you do your best.

Stella: (*Hopefully.*) Really?

Brutus and Tumbelina: (*In unison.*) Really!

Brutus: Let's pray and ask for God's help right now. (*Stella stands and forms a circle with Brutus and Tumbelina. With arms on each other's shoulders, they lower their heads.*)

© 2004 Gospel Light. Permission to photocopy granted. SonGames 2004 *Assemblies and Skits Production Guide*

Joe: (*To audience as if to a camera.*) This team is really starting to work together! Let's hope Stella is able to keep on with the competition.

Announcer: Next up: The 800-meter women's division race.

Tumbelina: (*In perky cheerleader voice.*) Come on, Stella! This is it. The race is about to start. (Stella *limps to the starting line, testing her ankle. She looks up and smiles. Three Additional Runners* enter from different directions and hold their noses, reacting to the smell of the muscle cream as they get into position.)

Joe: This is history in the making, folks! After some advice from her teammates, Stella Swift has decided to run in this final and longest race, the 800-meter.

Announcer: Get on your mark . . . Get set . . . GO!

(*Racers run in slow motion around the assembly hall, following the action and using facial expressions to show emotion as* Joe *narrates.* Tumbelina *and* Brutus *watch and react.*)

Joe: Stella pulls out of the blocks looking strong. (*Pauses.*) The other racers are keeping the pace. (*Pauses.*) Uh oh, it looks like Stella is struggling a little. (*Pauses.*) The runner from Slovakia is in first place, Sri Lanka is in second, Somalia is in third place, with Smallvania a distant fourth. (*Pauses.*) But wait. (*Excited.*) It looks like Stella's pulling into third. She is! (*Pauses. Disappointed.*) Now she's slipping back into fourth. (*Pauses. Excited again.*) Now she's in third again . . . no, make that fourth . . . no, third . . . no . . . no . . . oh, NO! Just steps before the finish line, the runner from Somolia takes third place! Slovakia wins, followed by Sri Lanka, Somalia and finally Smallvania. I can't believe it! Stella Swift lost a race! (*Play sound effect Cheering Crowd.*) Let's see if we can talk to her. (*Runs over to her.*) Stella! Stella! Can you tell our audience what it feels like to lose a race you were expected to win?

(Tumbelina *and* Brutus *congratulate the other athletes, who then exit.* Tumbelina *and* Brutus *then wait proudly during interview.*)

Stella: (*Breathlessly.*) I don't think of it as losing. (*Pause.*) In fact, I've never felt better after a race! (*She breaks into a big grin.*) You see, after injuring myself this morning, I knew I didn't have a chance to win. I didn't want to even try! But my teammates from Smallvania rallied behind me and told me to KEEP ON trying. I learned I can't always win, but I can ALWAYS do my best. I'm just thankful and thrilled I could finish the race.

Joe: You put out a real effort, Stella! You persevered, you kept on keepin' on, and you ran like the star you are!

Stella: Thanks, Joe! Now I've got to get back to my teammates. We're helping Tumbelina with her gymnastics routine for the competition tomorrow. (Stella *turns and limps toward her teammates and then turns back to Joe.*) Ya know the letters on our uniforms? (*She points to them.*) Be sure to ask me about them tomorrow. They'll look a little different. (*She winks at* Joe *and then limps to her teammates. They hug and congratulate her and then whisper together as they exit.*)

Joe: (*To audience as if to a camera.*) Well, like the great Yogi Berra used to say, "It ain't over 'til it's over." Be sure to join us again at the SonGames. Will Team Smallvania all go home victorious? I have my doubts, but they'll give it their best shot. That's it from the SonGames Sports Stadium. Sayonara [si-uh-NAHR-ah]! (*Joe exits.*)

Summary

Stella wanted to quit the race because she hurt her ankle and she didn't think she could win. What did Brutus give her to help her ankle? (Muscle cream.) **Tumbelina and Brutus reminded Stella that God would help her and be with her. This helped Stella run the race to the finish!** Give volunteer Session 4 Motto Pennant or reproduction to hold up. **Today we'll talk about how to . . .** Pause for students to shout "Keep On!" **trusting God when we have tough problems.**

Bible Memory Verse

In the Bible, God promises to be with us, to strengthen us and to help us. Open Bible and read Isaiah 41:10 aloud. **The next time you have a problem, remember that God promises to be with you!**

Prayer

Dear God, thank You for Your promises. Please help us to remember to keep on depending on You when we have tough problems or when we are afraid. Thank You for always being with us. We love You. In Jesus' name, amen.

Song

Sing "Do Not Be Afraid."

Announcements/Dismissal

Explain procedure for Session 4 and dismiss children to classes.

CLOSING ASSEMBLY

(10-15 minutes)

Materials: Bible, *SonGames* songbook and CD, CD player, word chart for "Do Not Be Afraid," Session 4 Motto Pennant or poster-board reproduction, SonGames Medals (see p. 4).

Play songs from CD as children gather. Give Session 4 Motto Pennant or reproduction to a volunteer to hold up during assembly.

Song

Sing "Do Not Be Afraid" from *SonGames* cassette/CD.

Prizes

Distribute SonGames Medals and/or other prizes (for more information, see p. 4).

Review

God promises to help us to keep on when things get tough. Invite everyone to recite Isaiah 41:10 with you. **What does "dismayed" mean?** (Sad. Discouraged.) **In today's Bible story, everyone on the ship might have been dismayed, or discouraged. Paul wasn't dismayed, or discouraged, because he knew God was with them and would help them. God is with us and will help us when we are afraid, sad or discouraged, too.** Have volunteer show Session 4 Motto Pennant or reproduction. **What is our motto for the day?** ("Keep On!") **Knowing this promise helps us to "Keep On!" believing in God's help, even when it is tough.**

Prayer

Dear God, thank You for Your promises to us. Please help us to remember to keep on trusting You when we are afraid, discouraged or sad. Thank You for sending Jesus so that we can become members of Your team. In Jesus' name, amen.

Announcements/Dismissal

Make announcements and invite children back for the next session. **(Tomorrow) is the last session of the SonGames. We're going to discover different reasons to celebrate. And then we're going to celebrate all (day)!**

SESSION 5

OPENING ASSEMBLY/SKIT

(10-15 minutes)

Materials: Bible with marker at 1 Corinthians 15:57, *SonGames* songbook and CD, CD player, word charts for songs "Join In!" and "Thanks Be to God," costumes for characters (see pp. 7-8), items for stage setup (see pp. 9-10), props (see p. 15).

Preparation: Set stage as directed in "Stage Setup" (see p. 13). Place sheets of white paper and markers on table. Place in cardboard box: Motto Pennants or reproductions, rolled-up paper scroll, inflatable globe ball, Runner's Torch, gift package with "Thank you" printed on it in large letters. Place white cloth, cardboard box and bicycle with training wheels offstage right. Place Flip Sign under bench. Hand handkerchief to Joe who puts it in a pocket. Tape, pin or sew "ER" Patches to Stella's and Brutus's uniforms, changing H.E.L.P. U.S. to H.E.L.P.ERS. Give each Judge two Scorecards: the first receives a 1 and a 10; the second receives a 2 and a 10 and the third receives a 1 and a 10. Give microphone, cosmetic powder puff and empty squirt bottle to Stagehand.

Play songs from CD as children gather.

Welcome/Song

Lead children to sing "Join In!" **Welcome to the final session of the SonGames. What an exciting (week) it has been!** As you say each of the mottoes that follow, pause and signal students to repeat them. **We've learned to "Join In!" "Team Up!" "Get Strong!" and "Keep On!" And so have our friends on Team Smallvania.** (Optional: Do twirl and *S*-team pose.) **Now let's watch to see if Brutus, Tumbelina and Stella find a reason to "Celebrate!"**

Cue *SonGames* CD to "SonGames 2004 Fanfare" or instrumental track of your choice.

Skit Script

(*Joe enters with Stagehand and moves to center stage. Stagehand preps Joe.*)

Director: (*Offstage.*) We're live in 5 . . . 4 . . . 3 . . . (*Stagehand thrusts microphone into Joe's hands, gathers props and hurriedly exits.*) 2 . . . 1! (*Joe smiles broadly and turns to audience as if speaking into a camera.*)

Joe: Bienvenudo [bee-ehn-veh-NOO-doh], bienvenue [bee-ehn-veh-NOO] willkommen [VIHL-koh-mehn] and WELCOME to VBSN's final broadcast of the SonGames.

(*Optional: Show video highlights [see p. 4 for more information].*)

Joe: We've been providing exclusive coverage of the team from Smallvania. This underdog team has become known as the wonderdog team! Their weight lifter, Brutus Liftsalot, and their runner, Stella Swift, have both won medals. Let's see if their gymnast, Tumbelina Turnover, can win a medal. But frankly, folks, it's a long shot, a real long shot.

(*Brutus and Stella enter from stage left, talking together. They are hurried, as if on a mission.*)

Joe: Let's talk to other members of Team Smallvania to find out what they think about Tumbelina's chances. (*Calling out.*) Brutus! Brutus!

Brutus: (*Brutus and Stella hurry past Joe.*) Sorry, Joe. Can't talk right now. I've got work to do.

Joe: (*Surprised. He turns desperately to Stella.*) Stella? Stella? How about you?

Stella: Sorry, Joe, but I can't talk either. I need to rent a bicycle.

Joe: Rent a bicycle? Ha! Don't have enough nerve to stick around and watch Tumbelina go down in defeat?

Stella: (*Stops for a moment as Brutus exits right. She turns to Joe, protesting.*) No! I WANT to watch her. I'll be right back. (*Exits stage right.*)

Joe: (*Puzzled.*) Rent a bicycle? Wants to watch Tumbelina? Is this the same Stella Swift who wanted nothing to do with her teammates from Smallvania just a few short days ago? (*Flustered, he struggles to fill air time.*) Uh . . . well . . . let's take a commercial break; we'll be right back with more live action from the SonGames. (*He feebly tries to smile. Then dropping the smile, calls angrily offstage left.*) Hey what's going on here? I was supposed to do a live interview with Tumbelina's teammates before she performs. Now we've got a lot of time to fill. What do you expect me to do?

© 2004 Gospel Light. Permission to photocopy granted. SonGames 2004 *Assemblies and Skits Production Guide*

Director: (*Offstage. Joe reacts with facial expressions of irritation and annoyance and then pleasure.*) Hey, like you say, Joe, sometimes you have to step up to the plate, crank it up a notch, dig deep. You've been begging all week to talk about YOUR glory days. Well, here's your chance. We're back on air in 5 . . . 4 . . . 3 . . . 2 . . . 1.

Joe: (*Joe brightens.*) Welcome back, folks. Joe Gabbyola, here. We're waiting for the start of the freestyle gymnastics competition. You know, back in the days when I was a professional athlete—

Brutus: (*Enters from right, rushed. He interrupts.*) Excuse me, Joe, you wouldn't happen to have a safety pin?

Joe: Yeah, I've got one on my press pass. (*Joe takes pin off his press pass, hands pin to Brutus and puts pass in his pocket. Brutus hurries off, stage right.*)

Joe: Well, as I was saying, back when I was a pro athlete, things were really tough—

Stella: (*Enters from stage right and runs up to Joe.*) Excuse me, Joe. You wouldn't happen to have a handkerchief?

Joe: Uh, sure, Stella. (*He pulls it from his pocket.*)

Stella: (*Stella takes handkerchief and runs off, stage right.*) I'll get it back to you later.

Joe: (*Still focused on his story.*) So, I was telling you about what was arguably the biggest win of my sports career—

Tumbelina: (*Enters from stage left.*) Hi, Joe, have you seen Brutus or Stella?

Joe: They've been in and out of here several times. (*Annoyed, Joe points offstage right.*) I think they went that way.

Tumbelina: Thanks, Joe. (*Hurries off stage right.*)

Joe: Where was I? Oh yeah . . . the big game. Okay, now the star player had been injured, so I said, "Put me in, Coach. I'm ready to play."

Announcer: (*Offstage.*) Attention all gymnasts! Please stay in the arena. We have one more competitor. The awards ceremony will follow thereafter.

Joe: (*Dejectedly.*) Well, so much for my story. (*Trying to rally up some enthusiasm.*) Okay, folks, it's crunch time for Team Smallvania. Can Tumbelina pull off a big upset? Don't bet the farm on it, Brutus! I need to remind our viewers that there are few established guidelines in the new competition of freestyle gymnastics. Half the score is determined by the technical difficulty of the gymnastic routine and half the score is for artistic expression. (*Brutus and Stella enter from stage right carrying cardboard box, placing it downstage right.*) It looks like the Smallvanian gymnast's teammates have set out a box of equipment. This is it. It's now or never, and probably never, for the gymnast from Smallvania! (*Brutus sits on bench. Stella removes scroll from box and stands in front of bench.*) Let's watch!

(*Play "SonGames 2004 Fanfare" or instrumental song of your choice during Tumbelina's routine, repeating as needed and stopping at the end of the routine.*)

Stella: (*Clears throat and turns to address the audience. Pretends to read from scroll.*) "A SonGames Celebration," created by Tumbelina Turnover. (*Tumbelina rides in on bike, wearing white cloth as a toga over her clothes, Joe's safety pin at the shoulder. Throughout her routine, Tumbelina uses exaggerated, dramatic and not necessarily graceful moves.*) The spirit of the SonGames is in a bike race, a gymnastics competition (*Tumbelina jumps off bike and does a somersault.*), rowing (*Tumbelina stays on floor to pantomime rowing.*), swimming (*Tumbelina pretends to swim.*), archery (*Tumbelina stands and pretends to shoot an arrow.*), baseball (*Tumbelina pantomimes swinging a bat.*), tennis (*Tumbelina pantomimes swinging a racket.*), track and field (*Tumbelina runs in place, does another somersault and comes up in a fencing pose.*), fencing and so much more. (*Brutus reaches under bench to get Flip Sign and then holds it up to read "Much More."*)

This great tradition started centuries ago, before Jesus was born. (*Tumbelina pantomimes rocking a baby.*) The people of Greece (*Brutus stands up and holds up Flip Sign to read "Grease." Stella looks at it, rolls her eyes and shrugs.*) started a contest that would inspire generations to follow—the Olympics. (*Tumbelina does a fancy little twirl, reaches down into her box and pulls out Runner's Torch.*) But even before the Olympics began, people would meet to compete. One such event was a race that runners started at sunset and ran in the dark. (*Tumbelina runs around stage in slow motion, carrying the torch.*) The torch was used to light the way for the runners to follow. People lined the streets to cheer the runners on and celebrate. (*Tumbelina waves and smiles at imaginary cheering crowds as she runs. Stella hands Brutus the scroll and sits down.)*

Brutus: *(Pretends to read from scroll.)* Today, athletes from all over the world *(Tumbelina reaches into box and takes out inflatable globe ball and balances it on her outstretched arm; then she dribbles it, tosses it up, catches it, etc.)* come together to celebrate the spirit of sportsmanship and competition at the SonGames. *(Tumbelina puts ball in box.)* Sometimes the games are filled with the thrill of victory and sometimes the agony of defeat. *(Tumbelina does a big jump of joy and then an agonized fall to the floor, pulling Joe's handkerchief from her sleeve to wipe her eyes and blow her nose.)* But the spirit of the games lives on as people cheer on the winners. *(Tumbelina waves handkerchief as if to a crowd. Stella pulls Motto Pennants or reproductions from box.)* The athletes learn to Join In! *(Tumbelina cartwheels; Stella holds up appropriate pennant.)*, Team Up! *(Tumbelina cartwheels; Stella holds up pennant.)*, Get Strong! *(Tumbelina cartwheels; Stella holds up pennant.)*, Keep On! *(Tumbelina cartwheels; Stella holds up pennant.)*, and finally, Celebrate! *(While Stella holds up pennant, Tumbelina does final cartwheel and stands wobbling, a bit dizzy.)*

Stella: *(Standing to join Brutus.)* And celebrate they do, when the last race is run. *(Tumbelina pantomimes running.)*

Brutus: When the last weight is lifted. *(Tumbelina pantomimes lifting weights.)*

Stella: When the last cartwheel has been cartwheeled. *(She makes a funny face about the line as Tumbelina does another cartwheel.)* They celebrate by giving gifts of peace and love to one another. *(Tumbelina pulls out gift box from box, holds it outstretched and moving it in a semicircle as if offering it to everyone, and attempts to go down into a split, holding gift box over her head.)* Here at the SonGames, before the torch fades, let's remember to be thankful that these games brought us together as teams and teammates. Not only that, but we also have the opportunity to become members of a greater team—God's team! *(Stella and Brutus step to either side of Tumbelina and help pull her back up. They put their arms around her. Play sound effect Cheering Crowd.)*

Joe: Wow! Was that emotional or what? What a performance by Tumbelina from Team Smallvania! It's up to the judges now. You can see them thinking this over. *(Judges are busy looking at papers, chewing on markers, etc.)* Gymnasts can get anywhere from 1 to 10 points for technical difficulty and 1 to 10 points for artistic style. She needs a total of 34 points to take home a medal. Let's see what the judges have to say. *(Judges are ready to hold up scoring cards on command.)* For technical difficulty, the judges give her: 1, 2, 1. *(Speaking frankly.)* Oh, those scores aren't very good. That gives Tumbelina a total of 4 points. She'll need three perfect 10s in artistic style to win the bronze. And the judges say *(Judges show cards one at a time.)*: 10! 10! 10! *(Play sound effect Cheering Crowd. Brutus and Stella rush forward to hug and congratulate Tumbelina.)* She's done it; she's won the bronze medal! Team Smallvania has another reason to celebrate. Tumbelina, what do you have to say? *(Joe pushes microphone in Tumbelina's face.)*

Tumbelina: *(Speaking through tears.)* I'm just thankful that I have great teammates who helped me and believed in me.

Joe: Stella, yesterday you told me to ask about your team motto. I see that it's changed to H.E.L.P.ERS. What inspired the change and what does it mean now?

Stella: It means just what it says! We're helpers now. I've learned that it's not as important to be a star as it is to help others. I'm proud to be a member of Team Smallvania and proud to help my teammates in any way I can.

Brutus: And I've gotten stronger here at the SonGames. I'm not talking about muscle strength but about the strength to keep on trying and to work together as a team.

Tumbelina: And I learned that listening to good advice from your coach and teammates can help you. I'm glad we all won medals, but the medals aren't as important as the friends we've made.

Joe: Well, you three sure make a great team. What an inspiration! Congratulations! *(Turning to audience as if to a camera.)* You saw it here first—Team Smallvania has become a lean, mean, winning machine! Well, that's it from the SonGames! This is Joe Gabbyola for VBSN sports. Thanks for watching, folks. Good-bye! *(They all wave and smile for a moment. Then Joe ad-libs with others, talking about his glory days as they exit stage left.)*

© 2004 Gospel Light. Permission to photocopy granted. SonGames 2004 *Assemblies and Skits Production Guide*

Summary

Team Smallvania finished the SonGames in a big way. Stella, Brutus and Tumbelina were all better athletes because of the help and encouragement they received from the other members of their team. They really had a great reason to celebrate! Today's official motto is "Celebrate!" God gives us His love, strength and help so that we will succeed at what is most important—loving Him and doing good things. His love is something we can all celebrate!

Bible Memory Verse

Let's read our Bible verse for today. Open Bible and read 1 Corinthians 15:57. **People like to celebrate victories. And this verse talks about the most important victory ever—winning as a member of God's team! What a great reason to celebrate!**

Prayer

Dear God, we thank and praise You for giving us Your love. Thank You for people who help and encourage us. In Jesus' name, amen.

Song

Sing "Thanks Be to God."

Announcements/Dismissal

Explain procedure for Session 5 and dismiss children to classes.

CLOSING ASSEMBLY

(10-15 minutes)

Materials: Bible, *SonGames* songbook and CD, CD player, word chart for "Thanks Be to God," Sessions 1-5 Motto Pennants or poster-board reproductions, SonGames Medals (see p. 4).

Play songs from CD as children gather. Give each Motto Pennant or reproduction to a different volunteer to hold up during assembly.

Song

Sing "Thanks Be to God" from *SonGames* cassette/CD.

Prizes

Distribute SonGames Medals and/or other prizes (for more information, see p. 4).

Review

Let's say our verse together. Lead students in saying 1 Corinthians 15:57 together. **We know God gives us His love, strength and help so that we will succeed at what is most important—loving Him and doing good things. All day we've been talking about celebrating.** Have volunteer show Session 5 Motto Pennant or reproduction. **We can celebrate the love and forgiveness God gives us as members of His team. We can be forgiven because Jesus died for us and rose from the grave. Jesus helps us choose to do what is right and live forever as members of God's team!**

We've had an exciting time here at the SonGames. And you've all learned some important mottoes about being members of God's team. What are they? Ask a volunteer to hold up each Motto Pennant or reproduction as you lead the children to say the phrases in unison.

Prayer

Dear God, thank You for loving us and sending Your Son, Jesus, so we can be members of Your team. Please help us to be good team members by obeying Your instructions and helping each other. Thank You for promising to be with us and strengthen us. In Jesus' name, amen.

Announcements/Dismissal

Remind children to invite their parents and friends to the Closing Ceremony. Children take home all projects and materials.

© 2004 Gospel Light. Permission to photocopy granted. SonGames 2004 *Assemblies and Skits Production Guide*

SonGames Closing Ceremony

Performance Preparation

As you prepare for the Closing Ceremony closing program, work closely with the Special Events Coordinator and the Music Director.

⚽ The Special Events Coordinator will organize all aspects of the closing program.

⚽ The Music Director will make sure children are prepared to perform during the Closing Program Skit.

- Preschoolers and kindergartners learn words and actions of "God Made Us." (Optional: Children learn words and actions of "God Promised.")

- Elementary children learn words and motions of "Join In!" "Teamwork," "Get Strong," "Do Not Be Afraid" and "Thanks Be to God." (Optional: Children learn words and actions of "The Lord Is God.")

- As described in the Session 2 Music Center activity (p. 5 in *SonGames Songbook*), groups of children prepare a cheer about teamwork. Select one of these groups, or form another group of volunteers, to perform the cheer as part of the Closing Program Skit.

⚽ Photocopy the Closing Program Skit Script (pp. 37-40) and give a copy to each actor in the skit. Rehearse actors alone and then rehearse entire production with all children before the actual performance.

NOTE: As needed, adjust the suggested staging (direction and timing of the children's entrances and exits) for the needs of your facilities and program. However you stage your program, it's a good idea to make sure children can easily view any videocassettes or slide shows.

Stage Set

Use the Stadium Backdrop, Sign Post, Standing Torch and Medals Podium (see *Elementary Teaching and Decorating Resources*). Place Sign Post at stage right and Standing Torch at upstage left. Set up Medals Podium at stage left.

Characters

The Closing Program Skit uses the same characters as the other skits: Joe Gabbyola, Brutus Liftsalot, Stella Swift and Tumbelina Turnover. These characters are described in detail on pages 7-8. In addition, there is an Official, who doesn't speak any lines but walks onstage to present medals, and an Announcer, who speaks offstage. These two parts may be played by the same or different actors.

Kid 1 has one line. Kid 2 and Kid 3 don't speak. Scene 2 calls for Cheerleaders, a small group that has a cheer prepared. Assign these parts to your most enthusiastic VBS kids!

Costumes

Joe, Brutus, Stella and Tumbelina are costumed as described on pages 7-8.

Props

The props needed for the SonGames Closing Ceremony include the following: handkerchief, two gold medals, one silver medal, three bronze medals. Give handkerchief to Tumbelina. Stella wears a gold medal and a bronze medal around her neck. Brutus wears a bronze medal around his neck. Give remaining medals to Official.

NOTE: Additonal props may be used during songs. See the suggested props on page 4 of the *SonGames Songbook*.

Closing Program Skit Script

Play *SonGames* CD as children and parents gather.

Scene 1

(Joe enters and turns to front, speaking to the audience as if speaking into a camera.)

Joe: Welcome, sports fans! I'm Joe Gabbyola, reporting live for VBSN television at SonGames 2004. We've gathered together tonight for the thrills and excitement of the Closing Ceremony. *(Joe looks toward back of auditorium.)* I see a number of the athletes heading our way now. *(Play "SonGames 2004 Fanfare." Stella, Brutus, Tumbelina and elementary children enter from back of auditorium. Children take their positions on stage as the skit characters stand together to one side, opposite Joe.)*

Joe: We've seen some mighty competitions here at the SonGames. We've seen the thrill of victory and the agony of defeat. And we've seen it all from the perspective of Smallvania's tiny team of tremendous teammates. Let's see if we can get a word or two from the members of Team Smallvania. *(He walks over to them.)* Hello, Team Smallvania!

Brutus, Stella, Tumbelina: Hello, Joe!

Joe: For those of you joining us for the first time, the members of Team Smallvania are weight lifter Brutus Liftsalot *(Brutus flexes his muscles.)*, runner Stella Swift *(Stella strikes a running pose.)* and gymnast Tumbelina Turnover. *(Tumbelina turns a clumsy cartwheel.)* How did it feel to be chosen to compete in the SonGames for your tiny country? Stella?

Stella: I was thrilled to compete as a runner, but I didn't want to be a part of our country's team. I'm used to training hard on my own.

Brutus: Yeah, Stella sort of had an "attitude." But she came around!

Stella: Brutus is right. I thought I was the star of Smallvania. *(Makes star shape in the air with her finger.)* But I found out that we are ALL valuable players.

Tumbelina: By the end of the games, Stella really joined in!

Kid 1: That's the first thing you do if you want to be on a team—Join In! Right, everyone?

All Children: Right!

Song "Join In!"

Elementary children sing "Join In!"
(Optional: Children sing "The Lord Is God.")

Scene 2

Tumbelina: Wow! That was awesome! Isn't it great that we can all be members of God's team?

Brutus: I was really glad that God gave me a teammate like you, Tumbelina!

Joe: And why do you say that, Brutus?

Brutus: Well, Tumbelina really encouraged me when I was so-o-o homesick.

Tumbelina: That's what teammates are for! We're Team Smallvania! *(She twirls around and strikes her S-team pose.)*

Stella: Yeah, Tumbelina kept saying that, and finally it sunk in. It's great to have friends who help me do my best! They really cheered me on in my races.

Joe: It WAS inspiring to see you all pull together. And speaking of cheers, next up is the SonGames Official Cheerleading Squad!

(Several students step forward to perform the following cheer, using motions they make up themselves.)

Cheerleaders: T-E-A-M
We're on God's team.
Living now
With love extreme.
God's our coach.
He guides the way.
Join In!
Team Up!
Get Strong!
Keep On!
Celebrate!
Celebrate!
Thanks Be to God!

Song "Teamwork"

Elementary children sing "Teamwork." ✶4 -18

Scene 3

Announcer: *(Offstage.)* Attention, please. The medals for the freestyle gymnastics competition will be awarded momentarily.

Joe: *(Facing audience as if looking in a camera.)* Sports fans, there's just one more set of medals to give out, for the new sport of freestyle gymnastics. In a surprise finish, the Smallvanian gymnast took third place. Tumbelina, before you take your place on the podium, please share with our viewers your experience here at SonGames 2004.

Tumbelina: At first I decided not to follow my coach's routine. I thought all I needed to do was take a deep breath *(Inhales deeply.)* and FEEL the moment. *(Tumbelina does a little twirl, tosses back her head and raises her hand over her head with a flourish. She pauses, holding the pose for for a moment as the others exchange quizzical looks. Then she breaks her pose and laughs.)* I almost blew my chance to win a medal!

Joe: What changed your mind?

Tumbelina: Stella and Brutus are great athletes because they follow their coaches' training programs. They advised me to follow my coach's instructions, too.

Song "Get Strong"

Elementary children sing "Get Strong." ✶5 -19

Scene 4

Joe: Now, Brutus, as Team Smallvania's weight lifter, you must know a lot about getting strong.

Brutus: It's true I've got a strong body. (*He flexes his muscles.*) But there are more important kinds of strengths to have. At one point, things started to go wrong for me. I lost my practice weights . . . (*Shuffles his feet, uncomfortable at the memory.*) and then I couldn't find my stuffed pig, Suey. (*He pouts and begins sniffling.*) And then I started to miss my mother's snufflejoodle—the best food in the world! And . . . I just . . . well, I just . . . (*He stomps his foot, bites his lip and tries not to burst into tears.*)

Tumbelina: It's okay, Brutus. Here. (*She hands handkerchief to Brutus who blows his nose mightily into it. Play sound effect Horn.*)

Stella: What Brutus is trying to say is that having a strong body isn't everything. Teammates can help us be strong; but more important, God helps us be strong, too!

Brutus: (*Pulling himself together.*) That's right! Even when we're sad, lonely or afraid, God is with us and He helps us!

Song "Do Not Be Afraid"

Elementary children sing "Do Not Be Afraid."

(*As song is sung, Tumbelina, Kid 2 and Kid 3 take positions on the medals podium. From offstage, Official enters, carrying gold, silver and bronze medals. Official places medals over the heads of the athletes. Tumbelina receives the bronze medal. Official exits.*)

Scene 5

(*Joe, Brutus and Stella gather around Tumbelina to congratulate her. During the following dialogue, preschool children enter, lining up in front of the elementary children.*)

Joe: Tumbelina, any reaction to winning a bronze medal? I'm sure you would have preferred a gold medal.

Tumbelina: (*Stepping down to join her teammates. Kid 2 and Kid 3 return to their original positions.*) Well, sure a gold medal would be nice, but sometimes winning a bronze medal—or even losing—can be a victory! Just ask Stella.

Joe: How about it, Stella?

Stella: Tumbelina's right. In my first race, I won a gold medal, just as expected. In my second race, I injured my ankle and only won a bronze medal. I didn't want to run my third race at all! I figured since I'd hurt my ankle, there was no way I could win. I didn't even want to try. But my teammates helped me and prayed for me. I tried my best and kept on. That's what made me a real winner—even though I lost the race!

Brutus: That's right! I'm glad I won a bronze medal in my event, but making new friends and knowing I'm a member of God's team are even better!

Joe: That's great! (*Facing audience as if looking into a camera.*) Ladies and gentlemen, I can see that the Junior SonGames Teams have joined us. Let's listen to what they have to tell us.

Song "God Made Us"

Preschoolers sing "God Made Us."

(Optional: Preschoolers sing "God Promised.")

Scene 6

(Preschoolers exit.)

Joe: Well, folks, that's it from SonGames 2004. There's one song still to be sung before the athletes go their separate ways. I can speak for all of us when I say that it's been a privilege and a pleasure to be here at SonGames 2004. For VBSN, this is Joe Gabbyola, wishing you all a good night and good sports.

Song "Thanks Be to God"

Elementary children sing "Thanks Be to God." Skit characters join in, singing song and doing motions.

Slide/Video Presentation (Optional)

Joe: Stay tuned for a special showing of VBSN highlights from SonGames 2004!

(Show slides or a videocassette of activities that took place during SonGames. Play songs from SonGames cassette/CD during the presentation. [Optional: Actor portraying Joe Gabbyola provides commentary.])

Closing

Leader or minister thanks parents for coming and invites them to learn more about God and His Son, Jesus, by attending other church events, mentioning one or two upcoming events planned for families. Leader or minister invites everyone to enjoy the refreshments (in the Fellowship Hall, on the lawn, etc.) and encourages everyone to meet at least one other family they didn't know before. Parents and students are dismissed after a brief prayer of gratitude.

© 2004 Gospel Light. Permission to photocopy granted. SonGames 2004 *Assemblies and Skits Production Guide*